WATER AND OIL

WATER AND OIL

A new concept of creation

NICK NEWTON

Copyright © 2020 Nick Newton
All rights reserved. No part of this book may be reproduced, stored, or transmitted by any means-whether auditory, graphical, mechanical, or electronic-without written permission of the author. Any unauthorized reproduction of any part of this book is illegal and is punishable by law.

To the maximum extent permitted by law, the author and publisher disclaim all responsibility and liability to any person, arising directly or indirectly from any person taking or not taking action based on the information available in this publication.

ISBN 13: 978-93-90025-07-7
ISBN 10: 93-90025-07-9

Printed in India and published by BUUKS.

CONTENTS

Acknowledgment ix
Prologue xi
Conflicts and Questions xiii

Chapter 1	The Start	1
Chapter 2	The Decision	6
Chapter 3	Power Grabs	12
Chapter 4	Return to God's Kingdom	21
Chapter 5	Phoenix's Arrival	26
Chapter 6	Anger	38
Chapter 7	Creating Extra Gods	42
Chapter 8	Warning	45
Chapter 9	The Great Flood	49
Chapter 10	The Cleanup	53
Chapter 11	Word Arrived	57
Chapter 12	Revenge from Earth	60
Chapter 13	Anger in the Heavens	63
Chapter 14	Search for the Dragon	65
Chapter 15	Phoenix's Return to Heaven	75
Chapter 16	A Solution Is Presented	77
Chapter 17	Sowing the Seeds	79
Chapter 18	Implementation of Plan Savior	82
Chapter 19	More Gods to Consider	87
Chapter 20	A New Plan	91

Chapter 21	The Arrival	93
Chapter 22	The Test	102
Chapter 23	The Battle	109
Chapter 24	The Challenge	126
Chapter 25	The Expansion	131
Chapter 26	Confusion and Doubt	141
Chapter 27	Conclusion	153

ACKNOWLEDGMENT

I would also like to thank Pravinraj-Sales Manager, for the great help and advice he has given in putting this book together. His company BUUKS and the other listed co-workers have been able to bring a difficult story together and turn it into a fascinating story. Ms. Sandra Sherin in helping with the cover suggestions and project coordination. Many thanks to you all for your very professional help.

    Phone   +81 800 8044 078 386
    Skype   ne.neel

PROLOGUE

Do you think a story can change your thinking or maybe even give you an entirely new perspective on an idea that possibly contradicts every account you have been told or has been told to you since you were born?

Could a new idea so entirely outside the usual stories and teachings over the last two thousand years. Could it be so different yet have the essence not only to be possible but also may be shown to be a more acceptable story than what most would believe possible?

I have related a story told to me over 20 years ago. During this time, I have spent many years researching trying to disprove or at least find a reason to discontinue the story as being just that, a story.

The truth is, I was unable to find any information that contradicted the story, which would have made it to be just that an exciting story yet a story from someone with a great imagination. Some may say impossible we have been taught entirely different ideas that have been set in stone, and any different stories must be a manifestation of the devil or worse his servants. Yes, the devil plays a very prominent role along with dragons, phoenix, the magical bird, and many other predawn creatures. Still, the actual meaning and conclusions will I am sure surprise and maybe even change your perceptions, which have been expounded from the beginning of human time.

After the long flight, I was so interested in finding more about the storyteller, and also I wanted to ask him a thousand questions. We got off the plane, and he was directly in front of me. Yet before we had reached the end of the passenger boarding bridge, I turned around to say goodbye to the hostess, then looking back, he was gone. Yes gone and no matter how hard I looked I never saw him again.

CONFLICTS AND QUESTIONS

Dear reader, whether you agree or disagree with the conclusions I arrive at through my story, I invite you to peruse through the conflicts and questions that I have enumerated here because they serve as the foundation to my story. One might recognize some Christian themes and story lines, as I narrate my story, but I am only sharing my story here, as it was told to me.

To begin with, what if everything Christians have been taught and believed in for over fifteen hundred years is not entirely true?

Why is this planet truly here? Are you willing to entertain new ideas when it comes to answering this question?

Even if you are a Christian and have a solid biblical foundation, it should be remembered that the Christian teachings as we know them today were disclosed to the public many years after the events took place, and sometimes the information was never disclosed.

Could it be that when we are taught about the beginning of the universe and the earth by the church we were totally misled as to how and why we are here?

The church hid many truths from the people during its initial establishment, which enabled them to have total control over their flock. They controlled the news, all information, and everything that happened in their congregations to the point of near-total acceptance by people that only the church was the source of all truth.

This allowed the church to exercise tremendous power and control over everything within their purview and label as satanic any new ideas introduced by anybody else. People who entertained or dared to believe controversial teachings that went against church doctrine were labeled as devil worshipers and put to death for heresy. (Note: Lucifer is the actual name given him as a spirit, but later he is referred to as the devil by the church and as Satan by Jesus, so all these names refer to the same spirit.)

Some of the most important inventions and discoveries during this period were claimed by the church to have been created or fabricated by witches, and many of these inventors were put to death or imprisoned till they admitted that they'd gotten their inventions or made their discoveries by worshiping the devil. For example, anyone who claimed that the earth was not flat, as was then believed, was either considered to be a fool or to be possessed by evil spirits. Many inventors, including great men such as Leonardo da Vinci, were told to stop inventing and describing their new ideas, on the penalty of imprisonment.

Even the written Word was withheld from the public and made available to those of high rank within the church, again giving greater control over the people.

Yet although people know the stories of how the church insisted that they were right because God told them so, no one questions the teachings of the church or even tries to sit down and ask whether it could all be a lie or, at best, a very exaggerated belief, in order to safeguard their own wealth and position.

Yes, even today in our enlightened world, with the Internet so full of information, the church has hidden or, in some cases, destroyed ancient scriptures and never deviates from the words they've been using for fifteen hundred odd years or so.

Even when one of the most sacred items in possession of the church—"The Shroud of Turin" or "Turin Shroud" (Italian: Sindone di Torino, Sacra Sindone ['saːkra 'sindone] or Santa Sindone), which is a length of linen cloth bearing the negative image of a man alleged to be Jesus Christ of Nazareth (courtesy of Google), is proven scientifically to have been produced in the years AD 1300–1400, the church still is in denial, saying, "Science is wrong!" They still insist it is a picture of Christ.

They sit on the idea that whatever the pope says is right and must not be challenged, which is exactly the same stance that was taken when the church was founded and made into a huge commercial enterprise.

Moving on, if we begin with the book of Genesis (from the Latin Vulgate, in turn, borrowed or transliterated from Greek "γένεσις," meaning "Origin," and in Hebrew: אֶרֶב תיש, "Bərēšī̱t," meaning "In [the] beginning"), it is the first book of the Hebrew Bible (the Tanakh) and the Old Testament (courtesy of Google), and it explains how the universe was formed and why there were great fights between the spirits, who were the only forms of life (though different to what we know on Earth).

In other words, it shows how a spirit called Lucifer, who was the second most beautiful spirit and next only to God in his powers, refused to acknowledge God's Son as being higher than himself in rank and therefore would not recognize the Son as being better than himself, which resulted in him being cast out of heaven along with all the spirits that were in agreement with him.

This caused a great conflict then, and even today such an event creates grief, conflict, and heartbreak in a family—when the firstborn is overlooked in the family business—and, in fact, many times breaks the family into pieces.

So if this Genesis story which is the first written account of such a conflict, and we see it being manifested so many times in today's World, then surely it must have a basis of truth? Right?

"So where is this going?" I can hear some asking.

It comes down to stage two: the establishment of a planet called Earth.

CONFLICTS AND QUESTIONS

We are told in the Genesis story that God created the Earth, and great detail is given as to how it was created within a seven-day period.

The earth has been floating around for about 4.5 billion years, per the scientific information we have today. But the book of Genesis, although not dated, is quite a new writing when compared to the actual time the earth has been around in this universe.

However, it was the first book of the Hebrew religion, which is really the first religion that we know of to believe in one God as the savior of the world. It is, however, important to remember that there were many man-made gods prior to this time.

Why would God need to be a savior when he created this planet? I will ask this question again later.

History makes many references to dragons. Are they just stories? More on this later.

Let us briefly digress and examine some ancient stories and beliefs, perhaps from about ten thousand years ago.

First, let's look at the Incas in South America. They had various gods and beliefs to cover most activities from birth to war. Human sacrifice was common, and the head priests again were able to create enough new gods whenever they decided the people needed a distraction.

The Egyptians had a different god for nearly every activity, from love to war: the priests and priestesses created the gods to be accepted as gods worthy of worship. Interestingly, none of these created gods was ever created by a being recognized as God; they were always created by humans claiming the power to make a new god!

In India, many gods were established to help the people accept their poverty and give hope to many, with various ideas and beliefs of how to get to a place called heaven.

So, at this moment in our short history, there were many gods being considered as being able to grant wishes long before the Christian beliefs surfaced.

Is it likely that if the spirits in heaven decided that they would like a new god to worship, they would be able to create one? Would not the only God of heaven and his Son be very angry if such an event were to take place? Would they allow it?

If the God of heaven would not allow such a thing in heaven, then if he did create the earth, why would he allow false gods here?

Does God need two places to get people to believe in him? Isn't one heaven enough?

It is also interesting to note that Jesus has been the only person ever to state that he is the God from heaven; in fact, he is the only one to ever claim that he is and always will be, whereas every other person, from Buddha to Muhammad and in-between, has claimed to be a prophet representing God.

Let us suppose that maybe, just maybe, God did not create Earth but that it was Lucifer who created it when he was banished from heaven, or as my story refers prior to being banished from heaven? Lucifer actually challenged God that he would one day control the universe—a simple statement—but could this place which is known as Earth be the challenging ground to gain power and one-day challenge God for the control of heaven?

Could the final showdown between good and evil actually be here on this planet and between the two most powerful gods in the universe? We are told in the scriptures that a showdown will happen, and I believe most have assumed the final conflict will be in the heavens, but we are also informed that Lucifer will be banished to total darkness.

Could that darkness be this planet when the sun is put out and this planet is turned into a solid block of ice?

Is it possible that we are here to challenge the forces of evil and march to heaven after our victory over evil?

Whom do humans blame for tragedies, close-family deaths, floods, earthquakes, and the many natural disasters that seem to be standard fare on Earth?

Why do we ask God to help us get through the wars but seldom ask him to stop the conflict and just ask him to help us as individuals?

Has the devil been given the credit for any tragedy or, in fact, for anything good or bad? This one question hints that the devil and his followers here are winning the battle between good and evil at this moment.

We are taught that the reason humans need to be baptized is that we were born with original sin. Yet how can a baby have any sin as we know it?

Perhaps we were originally created by Lucifer and his demon powers with a completely different agenda and baptism is maybe the only way to remove the stigma of Satan's powers?

We are told by the church that Satan has a fear of holy water. What if the devil has a fear of fresh water and he is afraid to go near fresh water? Would that explain why Christ baptized people in fresh water and why Christians today baptize with fresh water in the church? Although there is more salt water on this earth, it is never used to baptize. Could that be a reason?

The original story of Adam and Eve tells us one thing: if nothing else, on this planet, evil and its practitioners do and did exist.

Christ was tempted in the desert, and he could not banish Satan from this earth but could only fight his temptations. Surely if Satan was not here first, Christ could have banished him then and there?

Satan told Jesus to bow down to him and that he would then give him all that was here. How could Satan make such a statement unless he had control of this planet?

Genesis tells us a story of Adam and Eve being put into a garden called paradise, yet no one has any logical reason as to why they were kicked out of this garden; instead, we are told a story of Eve being tempted by a snake whom we refer to as Satan.

Although we are told that God is merciful, according to the story, are we to believe that Adam and Eve's first mistake is punished with banishment from paradise. Does this story truly have any logic?

Could this be what is referred to as Original sin? If so, are we completely missing both the teaching and the meaning of this thing called "original sin."

Was this first place called paradise actually created by Lucifer as a challenge to God that he could win any conflict with humans and, did he, in fact, actually win the conflict?

If we really look at this position with an open mind, surely it makes sense that we may have been duped for the last fifteen hundred years, right?

It is a fact that if a lie is repeated long enough and often enough, it will become a fact in people's minds. So where is the logic in a story that two people created by God are judged so harshly for one mistake?

The next question is this: Why would God send his only Son to a place called Earth to save souls he originally created?

If God is all knowing, as we are assured is true, and if he has the greatest power in the universe, he would have known as soon as he created a soul if he or she would turn against him. So why would he create a bunch of humans he knew would go against him? When Jesus picked his disciples, why did he pick two who he said would betray him before he went away from this world?

Was this a sign for future humans to give a message that he does know all things.

God already has heaven; if Earth were his, what would be the gain by having two places to control?

Could heaven be riddled with false gods to see if God was actually in control? If this could even be considered for a nanosecond, heaven would not be heaven; I am sure you'll agree with that.

It could also be asked, "Well, if God did not create Earth, why can't he just get rid of all evil powers here and let us enjoy a short but happy life?" We sadly do not have all the answers, but we are told that it will happen, yet not at our timing. Only God has that piece of the equation!

Sadly, it also has been stated that after Jesus was crucified, God was so deeply upset that he also indicated he would not directly interfere again in our affairs till the last days, but he did not say he would not help; he would help through others. This may be suggesting that unless it is absolutely essential to his plan, he will not again directly interfere, as he once did, as stories are told about the past.

There were gods, from Poseidon to Zeus to Neptune, and the list goes on and on, but really if we believe in the early writings as being a possible picture of what happened in our past, who do you think created all those gods and why?

It is interesting to note that most of the created gods seemed to have been either defeated or laid to rest so as not to cause problems in our present-day activities, but have they?

CONFLICTS AND QUESTIONS

Were they once real or just stories? But if they were just stories, why have they lasted thousands of years with no one challenging the stories? From China to England, we have stories of dragons, even a story about a guy named St. George, who actually killed a dragon, which is still considered real today. Is this fact or fiction? If fiction, why does the story still hold?

Written information of the church, during the many inquisition periods claims that witches had demons in them and were able to summon amazing powers from Satan (the devil or Lucifer). Could this be true?

The first written information regarding witches is from around 931 BC to 721 BC (courtesy of Google), well before Christians come into the picture.

Are we to dismiss such claims as not true and just stories?

We believe Christ was crucified on a cross, yet he was not the first to be killed in such a way. Crucifixion was invented by the Persians in 300 BC to 400 BC and developed, during Roman times, into a punishment for the worst of criminals. The upright wooden cross was the most common technique, and the time the victims took to die would depend on how they were crucified (courtesy of Google).

As you can see, it was well established three hundred years before Christ was crucified. So why should it be so important that we somehow relate to it as being so horrific that we cannot forget? Could it be because we all relate to a Son being put to death in such a cruel manner?

Many of Christ's disciples, we are told, were in many cases put to death in much more ghastly ways. For example, Peter was crucified upside down, as he considered himself unworthy of being crucified in the same way as Jesus. Many hundreds in other countries were put to death on a cross, and over many weeks, they were splashed with boiling water and kept in freezing temperatures, making it far more cruel and painful than what Christ had to endure. Yet we remember Christ's crucifixion as being so horrific and cruel, and we can always relate to his death. How many other people who have been crucified can we remember by name? Once the world was preached as being flat, and I am sure if we lived during those times, we'd also have believed that it was flat! Is it not possible therefore that some or all the passed-down stories could be based on what was seen or experienced during that period?

The stories that relate to the oldest living people in those early days actually refer to over ten who lived close to one thousand years. Yes, one thousand years! Could you believe that? So age, as we know, has changed dramatically since then; it went down to between thirty and fifty years and is now climbing back to around one hundred. As you can see, age has no boundaries to move up or down, depending, I am sure, on the circumstances prevailing at the time.

The next part I would like to quickly mention is during Christ's short stay on the earth, prior to his crucifixion, he was asked many times to take control of the situation and become an emperor or ruler to bring peace and stability to the earth, and many times he was reported as replying, "This is not of my kingdom." And he made sure that others knew this place was not a bit interesting to him and that only the souls here were of interest to him.

His reply was very clear—that this was not his kingdom; his kingdom was with his Father in heaven, which had more than this world could ever dream of. Is this reply, the reply from someone who created this earth?

We seem to only have a short period of the history of Earth considering it has been here for over 4.5 billion years, and our average life-span now barely reaches a hundred years, so do we really know what is and what isn't possible? One of the oldest accounts of war or tribal conflict we have, is around 2700 BC, and we are still getting better at it!

Everything today is moving so quickly that we really do not have more than a few short glances to see what is really happening around us. Even when we do, our time to consider or think about anyone subject is seconds only, and our ability to retain the information is even shorter.

Since the church was established, it has divided into different branches, all claiming to represent God and his wishes, yet from the very early times, many branches of the church have been tempted and corrupted into things far worse than could ever be tolerated in our society.

Many such branches also seem to be protected from any prying eyes, yet they seem mostly, if not all, to have fallen to many diverse temptations. Could this happen in heaven? I am sure not!

Could this be explained by the old rule "Divide and conquer"? Is this the stronghold that God would like to represent him?

Could it be that although God asked for his Word to be spread throughout the world, each branch could be breached by powers on this earth that could not be fought against by God here on Earth?

Such a position, I believe, if considered with an open mind, would or could not be allowed by God if he created this planet!

Does this sound like a planet created by God? It is interesting to remember that Satan considers himself a god and, in his over exaggerated opinion, believes he can defeat the God of the universe.

So when such a story is told, sadly few will consider it or even believe it to be true, but it has stayed with me ever since I listened to it, and at times, I have timidly tried to tell it.

An interesting point to mention is that with all the various representatives of religion on this planet, there is only one main point of difference between them.

The difference is in what happens when you die. One side says to be good, and that if you are good, you may return in a more advantageous position on your next visit. Conversely, you are relegated to being a lesser creature on your next visit. Your only hope to better yourself is to return in a more advantageous position on your subsequent visit. It is referred to as reincarnation, but is it not interesting that we cannot remember what happened the last time we were here? So how is it possible to improve on what you do not remember or know?

Could this idea be a ruse just to try to control or frighten you into being good as long as you do not look any further and discover that there may be a real God waiting for you? Maybe reincarnation is just a story to help humans accept their lot and not complain! The other side states we are here for one life only, and we had better be good, or else we will be thrust into damnation!

This seems to be in conflict also with the idea that God is merciful and all forgiving. So why would any believer in God be thrust into damnation?

It is also interesting to note that all religions, regardless of who formed them, have basically the same teachings, even those established long before Christianity. They all ask to be good, but if you examine them carefully, that is the only difference between all of them.

The one exception is the teachings in the first book of the Hebrew Bible (the Tanakh) and the Old Testament (courtesy of Google), which basically states, "An eye for an eye"—the idea of revenge against all who dare to attack you.

Could it possibly be that Lucifer also knew Christ would come and so he desired to cause as much confusion as possible?

The scriptures say, "Ask and you will receive; seek and you will find." Why are we told this so many times if this place was created by God?

Yes, now I can hear it: "Which god?"

Why do we always blame God for our tragedies, problems, and anything else that does not please us? Have you ever heard anyone cursing the devil for tragedies of any kind?

I think most people have heard stories where some people have asked for and been granted desires or pleasures, provided they accept the devil as being the person to worship—stories that all seem to have a tragic ending but that see the gain asked for granted before their demise.

Are these stories also fiction, or could they also have some truth? Even operas have been composed on this. Could they all be just stories? The world, as we know it, is filled with tragedies with a few seemingly amazing survivors, giving us hope or a seemingly good reason as to why we should all still keep going and keep the race thriving.

This endless struggle of the race to survive, hardship, wars, floods, earthquakes, and the thousands of tragic stories that befall the human race—are we to believe that this is God's will? Or could this anger be created by the only spirit in the universe who has been banished from what is the real paradise?

Could all that is happening be the work of a loving God who wants to grant us a place in heaven, or could it really be a planet where a huge conflict will be staged or launched against the real God of the universe? We are again told that the so-called end of the world will see many false gods arrive to tempt even the hardest believer into following. Is this the logic of a God who created this place or rather a message from a loving God to be careful and believe in one God only, who is waiting in heaven for us?

There are stories that tell of help from God who appeared at times of trouble and who intervened in dramatic ways to save his believers, which are well documented, and even after so long, there has been no one to disprove the help given by God to his followers.

There are also stories of people being told to sacrifice their loved ones, and yet at the last minute, they were told not to do it.

Could the initial temptation have been given by the devil in disguise, pretending to be God, and when the person was prepared to do it, the actual power of the devil was neutralized?

This question we will sadly never know, but why would a loving God ask someone to sacrifice a loved one when he very firmly stated, "Though shall not kill"?

Again, if the stories are read carefully and with an open mind, the real meaning and the real conflicts—remembering that some details could have been altered due to translation—will bear out very clearly. Lucifer would be a very angry spirit and has a very vindictive soul, which could also explain why his very existence depends on conflict and revenge.

If the world is examined carefully, everything on this planet is about the strongest survivor, and nothing else matters—from the smallest creature in the food chain to the greatest, till you get to the superior beings, the humans. Here, it is the strong who prey on the weak, and this starts from the very beginning and goes right to the end. We are taught to just get what we want, and it is pushed so that the strongest make it, and everything else does not matter. On a global level, this then translates to who controls a country and what other countries can they control. Could a loving God create such a place that is so full of conflict, anger, and hate that even today countries are starting to flex their muscles because they have a sign that reads, "I want"?

Has this planet ever been at peace in total? I believe somewhere even over the last one thousand years, and maybe longer, there has been some conflict in some country wanting a new owner or religion to be forced on the people.

Do you really believe this is the will of a loving God?

Many other examples could be given, but the object is not to list every conflict to convince others but to try to explain that although my story at times may sound like a kid's story, it is explained in this fashion to make it understandable.

Also, it is merely a story that is different from what has been preached over the last fifteen hundred years by the church as a Christian teaching.

Who do you think created this planet called Earth and why?

CHAPTER 1
THE START

Back before there was time, as it is currently known, there was just space, which was occupied by spirits—some very powerful with awesome powers and others with little or just basic abilities—who wandered around at will. There were no boundaries, and if a spirit wanted to, it could go beyond the existing space just by expanding it. There was nothing that restricted a spirit from going anywhere.

Spirits could create spirits by just deciding to make a few more spirits. They thus increased in number. It was thought that by making more spirits, the new spirits could be commanded to look after their creators. The spirits then coalesced into groups. All wanted to be in charge, but as it happened, the more each spirit tried to show why it should be in charge, other spirits would rise to the challenge, claiming that their ability was greater and so they should be in charge.

The one thing no spirit could do or can do now was to destroy another spirit; as each spirit was energy, and a spirit could not destroy another spirit without destroying itself.

The situation was such that primordial space was occupied by a huge number of spirits, all claiming to be the greatest and thus causing conflicts, with no one spirit being able to control the state of affairs or bring about calm.

After things seemed to reach a stalemate, it was decided for all spirits to assemble for a meeting to decide who, if powerful enough, should organize all the spirits with allocated areas of space to do as they wished in their allotted areas.

My narrator stopped and asked, "Does this sound like a story you may have heard before?"

"Well, it has some similar ideas, but no, I have not heard a story like this."

So he continued.

It was decided that a competition would be held to see what type of home each spirit could make and the conditions each spirit would like to make. There were no restrictions, and each spirit was told they could create it anywhere in space with the conditions they desired. At the end of it, all spirits would vote as to which world was the best and the most interesting.

At this point, no spirit had any idea as to what would be acceptable; they all had only "space" to begin with. But they all were free to create anything within their ability and any conditions that would make their world stand out. Anything could be placed in or around each world, and all the spirits would visit each of these created worlds and cast a vote as to which world they considered the best to live on.

Each would then be the king of their created world, and the spirit who created the best world would become the king of all the spirits. It was thought that this would stop the spirits from fighting, as each would have its own world to control. So all the spirits went off to make their own worlds.

Some placed huge holes close to their kingdoms as a means of preventing others from coming near them. Some holes were huge gaps in space able to consume any spirit or world that came too close.

These holes are what people here refer to as "black holes," but the spirits refer to them as "space moats" created for protection. The worlds that were created also created energy-making forces known as gravity, which also had effects on other bodies, which caused them to spin in space in what was a never-ending circle.

There is no end to this space, as other spirits are still creating and moving even farther away from their original starting positions. Some are so intent on staying away from detection that they have even expanded past what was considered the end, but there is no end as long as spirits are able to expand the area of space. At this moment, we can see thirteen billion light years from Earth, and that is not the end.

Some worlds were always engulfed in constant storms that were created to make sure other spirits never entered. Some were made beautiful to look at but could only be used by certain spirits. This was because some spirits did not want others to visit or interrupt their world. Some spirits actually created other spirits in different shapes and with different powers to help defend the areas they'd created.

After a very long period, all the spirits said that their worlds were ready, and the competition was ready to be judged.

All the spirits assembled and started the long journey to look at all the worlds, both large and small. Some were similar to this place, and others were beautiful to look at in their various colors. Many of the spirits were very amazed at the created worlds.

Some sparkled like cut glass or diamonds, and others were hot and barren, but the spirits did not need air and did not feel hot or cold, so the conditions were not important to some. It depended on their ability to create and what they considered important. Each world was given marks, and all the spirits gave their judgments as to what they thought about each of the created worlds.

It took many spirit centuries for the total examination of the created worlds to be finally completed, and then a tally was made to see which world was voted as the best one.

After checking all the votes, it was decided that there were two worlds that appeared equal and that there should be a chance for each spirit to add or subtract conditions to make their world the best.

Again, all the spirits were summoned to judge the conditions added, and all set off to decide.

CHAPTER 2

THE DECISION

Again the spirits gathered, but the voting was the same equal votes for each.

The two main spirits each decided that a vote had to be cast, as there could not be two masters over the spirits, and it was then decided to have a vote by all the spirits as to whom they wanted to be the king of the spirits.

After much deliberation, it was agreed that the best and most perfect world was God's and that all spirits should accept God as the most powerful and beautiful spirit in the whole spirit world. God looked at Lucifer and said to him, "You are the second most powerful and beautiful spirit in the universe, and I would like you to share the power to look over our wonderful universe."

Lucifer accepted the position of second-in-command and was happy being next to God's side. All went well for a long time. All the spirits were happy, and the universe was calm and happy. After a time God called a meeting

THE DECISION

of all the spirits as he had an announcement, which he wanted all to hear.

All gathered excitedly that there was going to be an announcement that would affect the whole universe. God announced that he wanted a Son who would rule next to his side and be equal in all respects to him. Hearing these words, Lucifer was shattered. "My position will be ruined. I will be nothing better than a would-be-in-charge spirit!" he said. "I will never accept you as King and will never accept a command by your so-called Son. Never will I bow down to him or you again, as I have my own kingdom, where all will follow me and not challenge me or suggest that I take a second and now the third place."

He was asked if he would change his mind and join the king, and again the offer was refused by the younger spirit, who stated loudly, "Who would like to join me in my beautiful kingdom?"

According to the scriptures, nearly a third of all the spirits decided to join Lucifer leaving the remainder under the protection of God. Lucifer was requested by the spirits that followed him, that they retain their powers and abilities, which Lucifer agreed to but with the reservation that should they use their power against him, they would be banished from his kingdom and never be allowed back.

This carried a lot of weight because the spirits who followed Lucifer had turned their back on the rightful king God, which they thought would mean wandering through space with no place to stop or rest—a very powerful reason to follow Lucifer without question and not try to depose him. Also, their ability to create new worlds was canceled, and all they had were the powers given to most spirits but limited to be less than Lucifer's.

The spirit world is based on electricity and each spirit has an electrical charge which is quite small, but when the spirits join together and all are as one, their power is magnified by the number of spirits joined together. This power is then transferred to their leader, God or Lucifer. When the spirit world was creating worlds and judging who would be chosen as the most powerful spirit and recognized as God of the universe, seventy percent of spirits stayed with God. This huge number assured God had the power to make his area, which was named heaven last forever.

Lucifer on the other side had the power to make his kingdom last a long time but lacking the numbers did not have such power and has always been in a lesser position when compared to God.

The only way a challenge could be made either against God or Lucifer would require a huge number of spirits all with the same position to join together before they could even think of challenging either. The main problem for Lucifer was because God had actually seventy percent of all the spirits and Lucifer only thirty percent from the start God was already well ahead in numbers. Lucifer was blinded by pride and would not

THE DECISION

believe he could not beat God over time by creating more spirits to follow him.

Also, Lucifer banished many spirits from his domain in the beginning, when the barrier was opened and many more spirits made their way to heaven which also made God in a position to never be challenged again.

Lucifer was tricked by Jesus when he opened Lucifer's block which initially prevented soles from leaving his domain and God has a block against any leaving heaven. This gave God an additional huge advantage to a point it seems obvious, Lucifer can never win the battle for soles. In addition, from the start God had no limitation on time creating, so he could claim "my kingdom is forever" and Lucifer has a limit on his kingdom. Lucifer has a huge ego and believes he can obtain the extra power and be able to create forever. For this reason he has no problem thinking he can get to God's level and beat him in the future, because, should he get to such a level with soles worshiping him, he could make his domain also last forever which he can not achieve at this time.

There is one main problem and that is the sole or spirit must agree to follow and should that spirit be upset or angry that spirits energy is not transferred, so Lucifer was initially expelling any spirit that did not worship him.

His idea was that he would just make more spirits, but when humans reproduced, that spirit did not know any information about Lucifer so it could not be counted as a force. Also being a lesser spirit because its power was so small locating such spirits or even giving them a second glance meant many were lost or overlooked till they died and then Lucifer could find it easily.

That is why Lucifer keeps creating gods because any soul who worships his created gods are actually worshiping him. The story shows Jesus wanted everyone to hear his name and know who he was and only with such notice could that spirit even know about heaven. All of Lucifer's additional gods all said they would show how to get to heaven or be with God, sometimes when they tried, maybe up to seven times or when they worshiped Lucifer. This made spirits think they had to get back to earth as the only way to get to heaven. The problem Lucifer discovered was any spirit could actually now leave of their own free will and Lucifer can never stop them leaving. In the past, he blocked such spirits until they agreed to do as he commanded.

Things were created, animals were produced, and the seas were filled with every type of creature the spirits could imagine. Some were developed and placed for amusement, while others were created for protection, and all went as planned, with all being content with what they had. The spirits who rebelled against God had, however, sadly misjudged Lucifer. Lucifer wanted more—he wanted everything in his world and the universe to worship him for his beauty and power. So he decided to ask the spirits to take on a less exotic form and become what was the beginning of the human race for a certain period of time. The spirits, as humans, would lose their powers and the memories they had as spirits but would enjoy human-like feelings and also be able to do things they couldn't as spirits. When their time as a human being was up, they would become spirits again and remember all that they had done.

Many agreed instantly and were placed in various parts of the new world with the ability to enjoy human feelings and freedom. What was not explained to the spirits was that, as humans, all knowledge they'd obtained as spirits would be taken away. Also strange as it was, many spirits were given a color, which they did not know as a spirit. When they asked why it was explained that this way each tribe could be judged by what they did and not be confused with the others. Also, each spirit was given a finger mark in its body, allowing each to be identified by Lucifer to ensure everyone did what they were supposed to do.

CHAPTER 3

POWER GRABS

It did not take long before, as humans, the greedy traits of the spirits started to come to the fore: "I want this." "I want that," "I want to do this," and so forth. The more they insisted on what each wanted to do, the less they considered Lucifer, and when summoned to explain, he reduced the power of each one a little at a time as punishment.

This action caused further dissension and made many dislike the powerful Lucifer. Some actually openly went against him. Some were brought before him and were then sent away to space, while others were kept in chains or made to pay homage to Lucifer or face very unpleasant conditions.

The mistake made by Lucifer was placing a limit on the time available to be spent as a human, and that time quickly approached for Lucifer, who was unable to increase the time established of around a thousand years by him in the beginning.

At the start of the human existence, time was not a problem, and it was normal for humans to live for close to a thousand years, but Lucifer had great power and decided he would use his power to remain as a spirit and come and go as it pleased him. This allowed him to influence what was happening in his kingdom and yet still have the power he originally had.

He did have the power to reduce the time spent as a human, and when he had trouble, he actually reduced the time available to humans. During many conflicts, humans at one stage had very small lifetimes, and some tribes actually were reduced to living only up to twenty to thirty years, seldom achieving fifty. This also caused problems, because some tribes just vanished, as they could not produce enough prior to dying.

So Lucifer made a fine balance and set the time to between minutes to around a hundred. Now while spirits can never die or kill another spirit without destroying themselves, they had the power to destroy other things they created. This limitation throughout the universe creates a balance that cannot be ignored. There was no limitation on disposing of humans, as the spirit was not destroyed, only the outer body.

Now spirits can be sent to or retained by more powerful spirits and ordered to assist when required. Lucifer though was, at this point, very angry, as people were more interested in their own requirements and had little use for a king, who could not talk or give orders as a spirit or be seen.

He could influence the spirits of humans to achieve what was needed, but should that human be killed or, in fact, actually want his own direction, Lucifer lost power over the human, which made him so mad that he wanted to destroy all humans and return them to their spirit forms whom he could control.

Lucifer thought of another idea, and that was to ensure that each baby born would retain some fingerprint of the father, believing that such an idea would ensure loyalty to him, the king and god of the world. A huge problem was that humans who created other humans either could not be controlled anymore or could only be controlled with great difficulty. This weakened Lucifer's actual control to a point that his ability to give directions became harder and harder. The humans liked producing humans in a similar way that the original spirits liked to produce, which expanded the number of those who did not know the king spirit and had never heard of him or his ability. So to reduce the number of those who did not know him, Lucifer created wars and arguments and introduced greed to get rid of human spirits who were against him in his world. He banished these spirits to space without any ability to create their own world, and with no ability to return, they could only wander through space looking for a place to go, so he thought.

The humans varied in ability and knowledge, and some found ways to summon the spirits to assist them in achieving what they wanted and actually used the powers for self-gain.

POWER GRABS

The spirits that were summoned from the underworld by humans had more power and usually hid in other humans which was like hiding behind a mirror and even Lucifer had trouble seeing that a spirit was behind the mirror. He could only see the reflection of the spirit giving life to the human and seeing behind the mirror was extremely hard if the spirit did not want to be discovered.

If commanded by Lucifer to take over a human Lucifer could see his spirit clearly but only if he actually commanded the spirit initially. This way spirits could hide undetected by Lucifer until the human died and then the spirit had to hide until they could find another human or be caught by Lucifer and returned to where they came from. The problem with such a situation was that for Lucifer to see his rogue spirit he actually had to know which human the spirit was hiding. If the spirit could not find a human to take over, Lucifer could normally, within a short period find the spirit and return it to where it came from.

The additional trouble Lucifer had sometimes was convincing this strong spirit to stay with him because the spirit was free to leave if it desired to. Lucifer's power to retain spirits was removed when he arranged the crucifixion of Jesus, but that later.

The spirits brought back so that they could be seen were, in most cases, very mischievous and many times turned against their masters and caused much confusion to a point that many were sent back, and then the ability to call them back was destroyed so they could not ever be summoned again.

Some humans actually made secret writings so as to be able to bring back the spirits to help when required. These old writings were saved and kept so that other generations could get help if needed. Lucifer was so mad at this intrusion without his permission that he, at times, sent his own black spirits to attack the spirits that did not have his permission to act in his world. The spirits were attacked and then banished back to their rightful place controlled by Lucifer and forbidden to ever be called again.

These black spirits would do whatever was commanded by their master, they had amazing powers and could not only change shapes, become invisible and fly at amazing speeds when commanded, but also had the ability to take over a human, control what the human did and bring its demise when it left. They used the human like a parasite and drew their energy from the human's blood. When they left the human rather than be sent back to the underworld, would many times look for another human to take over. This sometimes became very hard as many humans could not be taken over or invaded so easily without the direct orders from Lucifer. However, the need for sustenance did not diminish and many times they would take the blood from unsuspecting humans usually when they were asleep. This could take days or weeks but when a human was found, Lucifer had great trouble finding his rogue spirit.

POWER GRABS

Monster animals were created and controlled by some to banish foes, and others were created to protect their areas from invasion from other humans. Some humans developed animals that could fly across the country and cause fear or attack other humans for material gains. Some actually managed to fly without any animals, and others developed skills to move huge rocks to build fortresses with little effort. Some humans developed skills known only to the spirits and gained great power, as many humans actually thought they were gods and would grant what they wanted.

This again caused conflict, and it happened, so that often Lucifer actually had to destroy the power used by some. He could not kill them, but by destroying their power, it limited their ability to cause trouble. Whenever the human population increased to a point that his power was diminished, he created a fight between tribes and always assisted the one he wanted to win. This kept his power for a time, but he always seemed to be fighting to just hold on to his power.

After a long time of trying to solve the problem, he decided to allow other gods to be created, which few knew were actually his created image so that he grew in power. For a time, he seemed satisfied, and many new races developed, each having new gods, but as they were actually his creations, he was happy.

There was also another problem emerging, and that was that although the spirits could not remember when they had become humans, they could remember when they returned to spirit forms. So how to keep the spirits happy and want to return as humans?

This was a huge problem, but Lucifer was a powerful spirit and also extremely smart. He decided to create gods who taught that when humans returned as spirits, they would believe the only way to become equal to God was to return in a lesser or greater form until they had achieved perfection.

This made the spirits believe this kingdom was the only way that perfection could be achieved, and they would never want to leave.

It must be remembered that few humans had any learning and were easily tricked by these so-called leaders representing different ideas and gods that had been carefully selected by Lucifer.

Everything went smoothly for a time, and again Lucifer thought all was in control and his power started to get stronger.

At this time, some tribes wanted to move and discover what this place was actually like and wondered whether there were better places to find.

Lucifer did not want some humans to move, so some landmasses were moved to prevent them from joining other forces that were for various reasons unaware of the power he had. These were called earthquakes and explained by stating that the gods were unhappy and that people should pay more attention to Lucifer or to the gods so that all would be put back to normal.

This worked and also explained any happenings that the humans encountered as being either caused by the gods or because of natural causes, but mostly it was because the gods had become angry or because Lucifer was unhappy.

Again, Lucifer gained power, but the number of spirits that were banished to space grew more and more, and also, the spirits who knew what was happening began to question Lucifer's motives in banishing so many. Little did Lucifer know that all the spirits banished by him found their way to heavens gate where they were welcomed.

The reason for such questions was that many believed that the only place they could become perfect was in this world, and by banishing the spirits away, it seemed that any chance to improve would be lost forever.

The population started to grow and spread faster than Lucifer wanted, so again tribes were encouraged to fight, and the bigger the fight, the happier Lucifer grew. The barbaric tribes were sent against the weaker tribes, spilling rivers of blood across plains, and some rivers ran red with blood from humans killing each other. It seemed Lucifer was pleased when blood was spilled, and the more it happened, the happier he became. In fact, Lucifer actually became sad if no blood was spilled; he became addicted to spilling blood and the power it created. When things calmed down and it became hard to start a war or conflict, he created more gods who demanded blood sacrifices just for pleasure. This grew in popularity and, in fact, increased his power, but it had a devastating effect on the people, who demanded younger and younger sacrifices, which eventually destroyed many of the tribes who practiced human sacrifices.

CHAPTER 4

RETURN TO GOD'S KINGDOM

Meanwhile back in heaven, a completely different situation had developed. There were no humans allowed; only spirits who had powers but never as great as God's which were able to join together and form groups with similar likes. The only conditions were that God was honored at all times and that no spirits would ever challenge his authority or rules.

As God's power increased, word spread around the universe that any spirits lost or wanting refuge could enter the kingdom as long as they recognized God as the one and only God.

As other spirits joined the kingdom, they also brought different powers and the ability to create different ideas. Now you might ask, "What can't spirits create?" Well, unless you know about something, it is very hard to imagine it.

This was the case in heaven. All spirits were not created with the same abilities or knowledge and could only obtain this knowledge after being shown or taught. All the spirits were created in the same way. They were similar, but each spirit was different.

The secret of heaven was that it was not limited to size or boundaries as was Earth and was able to expand and change as was necessary to please the spirits who were there and who at times even tried the patience of God by their creations.

However, other than creations such as flying horses, dragons that guarded the gates of heaven, the phoenix, the unicorn, and other mystical creatures, the kingdom was happy, and all the spirits were very happy to be there. Their power grew, and heaven had no limits to the happiness within it.

God grew stronger with the more spirits who accepted him as the one true God, and the more powerful he became, the more power he had to achieve happiness within his kingdom.

Some spirits had created their own kingdoms and also had spirits who considered themselves to be king, but no kingdom created had the power or happiness of heaven, and many spirits who had heard of heaven wanted to go there but were sometimes prevented by their kings. Heaven's gates were always open to any spirit who wished to stay, and the only condition was that they accepted God. Should they refuse, they were immediately set upon by the dragons and sent away, never to be allowed to return.

As time progressed, word spread in the heavens that Lucifer from the distant world had created a kingdom filled with bloodshed, wars, and famine and had made the kingdom a prison for all who were there. It was impossible to enter the world unless a human form was adopted, and the only way to leave was what the residents of the kingdom called "death." This then allowed a choice to be made: stay or leave.

It was forcing new spirits who did not know of any other kingdoms to either go to in space and hope for a kingdom to be found to accept them or stay in another form in this human world. It not only made the spirits fearful of wanting to leave but also made sure Lucifer's power became stronger.

Lucifer had also decided that another way to keep his spirits under his control was to now make it impossible for them to leave no matter what desires or wishes the spirits had developed. He had made a gate that prevented any spirit from leaving unless it was with Lucifer's agreement. In this way, any rebellious spirits could be kept away in separate areas so as not to be able to cause trouble. Also, it allowed Lucifer to decide easily what spirits should be allowed to return as humans and those who should never be allowed to reenter as humans.

Such news troubled God in heaven, as it was very hard to send help or in any way try to help the spirits caught on Earth, who were suffering for the total benefit and pleasure of Lucifer.

After some time, considering the presented problems that were happening on Earth, a meeting was called to discuss if help should be considered and if help was needed, then what type of help should be sent. The meeting was called, and the position was explained by God. "Maybe there are spirits in Earth who are prisoners and spirits kept in Earth that may need help. Would all the spirits discuss the problem and let me know what ideas you may have?"

It was decided that maybe the dragon, who had the power to fly faster than light, should go and see if anything could be done to help the people who were in trouble and report back to God on what was happening there.

The dragon was dispatched, and although he had magical powers in heaven, his powers were restricted. Even his ability to fly faster than any other spirit seemed to be reduced, making it harder to fly. Also, people were afraid of its appearance, and most ran away in fear, thinking it was a new god created by Lucifer that would eat them if they were caught by it.

Lucifer heard of this monster in his kingdom and immediately sent forces to find and capture the mysterious creature. The dragon had no fear but also limited knowledge of treachery and the power of Lucifer in this kingdom.

He was soon tricked, bound with gold chains, and taken away to be held captive inside a volcano, where his ability to breathe flames would be hidden from all. Even when he wanted to scream out in anger, all that came was fire and smoke, which the people said was just a mountain god getting upset over what the people were doing.

His cries for help were not heard, and after a long time, God asked, "Where is my faithful dragon?" "He has not returned," came the reply. "There has been no word or any indication where he is, and we are all worried." At first, God was not worried, as he knew the dragon had special powers, and surely that was enough for him to go and quickly return without harm. What he did not know was that the dragon's powers, for some reason, were limited, which made him an easy target on Earth, and that Lucifer had now captured him.

After some time, God summoned everyone to decide on what action to take in finding his faithful dragon. "Why not send the phoenix, as she can fly faster than the dragon and can use her powers to be invisible when she wants? Surely she can, with her ability to change shapes and fly so fast, find the dragon and return him here!" So now it was decided to send the phoenix to find the dragon and also discover what was happening in this planet called Earth and whether it was true that on Earth people were suffering for Lucifer's pleasure.

CHAPTER 5

PHOENIX'S ARRIVAL

Phoenix arrived on Earth but had trouble entering its realm, as an invisible shield had been placed around this place, which was to be a barrier against spirits coming or leaving; in fact, it made the entry extremely hard. Phoenix made herself invisible and after some time was able to find a small opening in the barrier, which allowed her to just squeeze through.

A problem she faced upon entering was that it was extremely hard to fly; it was as if someone had a line tied to her tail, so her ability to fly at her normal speed was impossible. As she looked like a longish bird, she flew high enough so as to not arouse attention, but few noticed. Now and then, she would touch down, take the shape of one of the humans, and ask, "Have you ever seen a dragon?" Each time she was met with the same or similar answer: "What is a dragon?" On and on she went. It was as if the dragon had just disappeared without a trace. Still not wanting to give up, she continued to search—up in the hills and down in the valleys, sometimes using her secret call, which she hoped the dragon would hear. Still nothing.

As she flew over the country, she noticed an old man out in the fields alone. Down she swooped and again took the shape of a human as if she was just passing through. She struck up a conversation with the old man and after a bit of casual talk, she asked, "Have you ever heard of a creature called a dragon?" The old man thought for a while and said, "Actually when I was very small, there was talk of a long beast that could blow fire. Would that be a dragon?"

"Maybe; I am not sure. I am interested to discover if such talk was real or just imagination. Do you know any others who may know if it was real or just a story?"

"Well," the old man said, "there is a very old person who lives in a cave over the next hill, and it is said, that person knows everything and even has the ability to see the future, but you must take care. They say that if the person does not like you or you do not have a gift, the person will destroy you."

"Thank you very much. I will go and ask because as much as I do not believe, I would really like to know if such a creature did exist."

"Good luck," came the reply as she quickly walked out of sight to return to her normal self.

Up she flew, and sure enough, just over a few mountains, she saw a cave, but what she saw told her that she had to be very careful. Outside the cave were several very large hyenas, each with two heads, lying outside the entrance, and as she flew by, they all sat up and started to look at her.

She landed on the hill and changed into a woman, similar to what the locals were wearing, and slowly made her way toward the cave. As she approached, the hyenas started howling and immediately moved to guard the entrance of the small cave.

As she approached, the hyenas became very agitated and started to growl and move together to make passing impossible. After some time, there was a command, and the hyenas moved aside. A person emerged—it was impossible to determine if it was a man or a woman, as the old blanket covering made it hard to make out a face or shape. In a loud voice came the question, "What do you want?"

"I would like to inquire whether a large creature called dragon ever existed."

"Why?"

"I have heard about such a creature and would like to know for sure if it is true or just a fable."

"It will cost you. Do you have a gift for me?"

"Yes, I have a special gift for you if you can let me come in and tell me the story." "OK, come in, but do not look at my friends at the door even if they act to bite you." She entered and was surprised to see how large the cave was inside, and although dark, she could see clearly everything inside the cave. What surprised her most was that on each side of the chair, on which this person sat, were two of the largest saber-toothed cats she had ever seen. Both of them started growling as soon as she entered, and in fact, they'd have grabbed her if it wasn't for the person's strong command forbidding the cats from doing so.

After some moments, the person looked up and asked, "You are not of this world. What do you want?"

A little surprised, she asked, "What may I call you?"
"You may call me Aradia."

"I have to find my friend, a dragon who went missing some time ago, and I would be very grateful if you could tell me what you may know about him or where I may locate him."

"What gift have you to give me?"

Reaching into her pocket, she offered a beautiful red stone, which glowed inside the cave to the amazement of Aradia, who held out its hand with obvious delight.

"Well, as you may know, our king does not like visitors from other worlds, and if anyone is caught helping or not informing the king, they are banished to space, never to be able to return. Let me see if there is news about your friend, but if you are caught, you must not mention our meeting. So you must assure me that you will deny knowing me and ever meeting me."

She agreed immediately, and with that, Aradia moved over to a large circular basin filled with what looked like water. She stared into it for several minutes without saying anything. She was about to say something but then stopped.

Looking over, she looked as if she was struck by lightning. "The king has reports of a strange person in his kingdom and is asking for confirmation, so we must be quick. Your dragon has been captured by the king's army and is held in a dark place filled with fire. You must leave now!"

"Where is this dark place?" Phoenix asked hurriedly.

"Under a mountain that is blowing smoke. Now please leave quickly!"

She immediately ran out and behind the hill, changed into her regular form and soared high into the sky.

Higher and higher she flew till she could see over great distances. After looking in all directions, she saw four mountains blowing smoke and decided she had to check each mountain to see if the dragon was actually there.

Turning herself invisible, she went as fast as she could to the nearest mountain, and looking down, she called out to the dragon to see if he was there. There was no response. Again she called out, getting closer, and again there was no answer. Swooping down for a closer look, she went to the top and asked in her loudest voice, "Dragon, are you there?" Again no answer. She flew to the next mountain, and again no answer. On reaching the third mountain, she saw another mountain blowing smoke and started to wonder if she had been tricked.

However, rubbishing that thought, she immediately flew to it, but again, there was no answer.

The fourth mountain was at a great distance, but she flew at the fastest speed she could manage and quickly reached it. Still, the same result.

Thinking that maybe the dragon was not in a mountain and feeling very exhausted, she went down to a forest to rest in one of the largest trees so as to not be seen, because she could not remain invisible when sleeping.

Soon she was fast asleep and dreaming about the dragon; she saw him in chains and roaring out in desperation for help. She immediately awoke and decided that as hard as it might be, she had to go to the next mountain, hopefully, the last mountain, to find and free the dragon. In the meantime, Lucifer had started to ask, "Has anyone heard or seen a strange person asking questions about a mythical dragon?" He was informed that a woman had been asking, and he immediately dispatched his army of black spirits, who looked like humans but could fly at great speeds and distances, to find this woman. They were to bring this woman to him immediately. Phoenix was also being very careful, and most of the time, she remained invisible when awake. Upon arriving at the last mountain, she looked down but could see nothing. Believing she had been tricked, she was about to go, when she heard the faintest cry from what she thought must be the dragon.

Although tired, she transformed herself into a human, but remaining invisible, and crept down the mountain, looking for an entrance. Sure enough, just as she got to the bottom, she saw several humans going in through a concealed entrance and immediately joined them as they went in.

All was well till she arrived at the cells being guarded by small flying dinosaurs with sharp teeth and very evil-sounding screams. They all started screaming at the same time, and the guards who could see nothing commanded the animals to lie down and be quiet.

She still could not see or hear the dragon, but she was sure he was somewhere near. So she went farther inside, and after a long time, at last, she saw the dragon chained to the wall, unable to move except for being able to blow flames through a tunnel leading to the main hole, which looked as if the mountain was blowing smoke like the other mountains. The dragon could not free himself from the chains by melting them because he could also burn himself, and if he damaged his back, he'd never be able to fly again.

When the dragon sensed that phoenix was near, he became quiet and tried to see her. In a soft voice, phoenix said, "Dragon, act the same way as you have been acting so that no one becomes suspicious, and I will see what can be done. Do you know who has the key to your chains?"

"Yes, the head spirit guard, who has huge powers, and it would be hard to get the keys from him."

"I will see what can be done, but do you know where he normally is and does he have any habits that I can take advantage of to trick him?"

"He has a big feast each night and likes his wine very much." "Well, keep doing what you have been doing, and I will see what can be done."

On returning, the dinosaurs again shrieked and screamed, and again they were told to be quiet. There was nothing wrong. The head guard was huge and walked with thundering steps, which were so loud that the ground shook, and when he demanded something, all rushed to his command.

"I feel hungry. Bring food!" he commanded, and immediately all rushed around to find his favorite foods.

The phoenix hid in his room while the food was brought to his table. When the wine was poured for him, she moved closer and turned his wine into a strong sleeping mixture with an amazing taste. He immediately started to drink and quickly drank many cups of the wine. After some time, he sat down and started to doze off to sleep. The phoenix saw the key to the dragon's chains, but it was so big and heavy that she thought she might not be able to lift it. And how would she get it past the guards?

The only way was to use all her power to make the key invisible, but this would also limit her power to stay invisible. But the dragon had to be saved, so she summoned all her power and made the key invisible. She was so tired that she could hardly lift the key from the guard's belt, and she also knew her time to remain invisible was limited, so she had to hurry.

As phoenix approached the gates where the dinosaurs were chained, dragging the key past them to get to her friend, she could feel her power to remain invisible fading, and the animals again started to scream agitatedly. The guards rushed out but could see nothing, so again they commanded the animals to be quiet in case they woke the head guard. Climbing through the bars was also a struggle, as she was in the shape of a human, but as it happened, the bars of the cell holding the dragon were slightly wider, allowing her to squeeze through the bars. The dragon was so happy to see his best friend that he became quiet, but the phoenix told the dragon to keep making noises. She was feeling very weak and also noticed that she was half-visible now, so she began to hurry. The lock was positioned high behind the dragon's tail, meaning she had to lift the key quite high to get to the lock. After many tries, she got the key into the lock, and the lock opened with a loud click. The dragon started to make louder cries to cover the noise of his chain dropping, and the guards immediately issued a loud command to the dragon to be quiet or receive a beating.

The phoenix was now a visible human form and very weak, so she told her friend that she had to revert to her normal shape or be lost forever. Changing back, she went behind the dragon and asked whether he could melt the bars enough for them to escape.

"Maybe," said the dragon, "but hide behind me, so the flames do not burn you." The dragon started to blow flames at the bars, but he also was weak from having been held captive for so long, and his flames were not very strong. But he kept trying, and finally, the bars began to glow red.

The cell began to get heated, and the dragon was worried that the guards would come to check what was wrong. The phoenix, looking around, noticed the top of the bars—which should have gone into the rock of the mountain—were held by huge wooden beams and a supporting bar; they would be impossible to move as a human, but the dragon could burn them down.

The dragon then started to burn the solid beams. The burning wood led to a lot of smoke, and the dragon was worried about the guards detecting it. But there was no turning back now. When the fire had sufficiently weakened the beams, the dragon wound his tail around the supporting bar and pulled with all his strength. The bar began to give way! After a few more attempts, the bar finally fell through with a huge crash making so much noise that the guards rushed to the dragon's cage.

The dragon told the phoenix to jump on his back and pushed through just as the guards approached. Up he flew with the phoenix on his back as the guards approached, screaming, "Stop, stop!" The dragon was quickly into the sky, but the guards released the dinosaurs to chase it. The dinosaurs could not fly very high, and the dragon belched huge flames at them, setting them on fire, and they fell burning to the ground. He asked the phoenix, "How did you get in? Lucifer had put a barrier, making it hard for spirits to leave."

"Yes," said the phoenix, "but I found a small hole at the top of this world, yet we must hurry because Lucifer has surely by now heard of your escape and will be looking for you." They approached the top and found the small hole, but it was not large enough for the dragon to get through.

The phoenix looked around, and sure enough in the distance, she could see black specks of something approaching. She said to the dragon, "See if you can burn a hole to get through because if we can get through, they cannot follow us or harm us, as they are bound to this kingdom."

Seeing them, the dragon again blew his hottest flames hard at the barrier. The barrier was very high up, and it was very cold at the height, so the flames were not as hot as when he was on the ground. However, slowly, the small hole started to get a little larger. "Yes!" exclaimed the phoenix. The dragon kept at it; the black dots were now getting larger—they looked human but were very large.

"Dragon, we must hurry!"

The dragon was still breathing fire toward the hole, and finally, it became large enough for both of them to squeeze through before the human-like beings could get close enough to cause trouble.

Arriving back at heaven, both the dragon and the phoenix were exhausted but went immediately to God to explain what had happened and how they were able to escape.

PHOENIX'S ARRIVAL

The dragon explained to God, that Lucifer had created gods in all sorts of shapes and sizes and had turned the humans against humans so they would kill and torture each other for Lucifer's pleasure. Also, Lucifer had changed their original traits so that all bad traits developed would be automatically transferred to any new humans created. This ensured that humans over time would desire only power and would eventually lead to them being totally controlled by their desires and needs instead of that of spirits. This would thus give Lucifer total control of all humans created; his kingdom would become a very bad world, and any help from other forces outside his world would be blocked. The dragon continued by also mentioning that Lucifer had blocked most spirits from entering his kingdom unless they actually became a human in form and ability, losing most, if not all, of the power spirits could bring into his kingdom.

God listened, and being very upset at the treatment his dragon had received and his report, decided to call a conference of all the other spirits to develop a plan that may allow some spirits to escape from Lucifer's rule if they wanted. However, what was troubling was that most humans had no knowledge of heaven or that it even existed, and it had to be figured out as to how to inform the humans on Earth of this.

CHAPTER 6

ANGER

Lucifer, on hearing that the dragon, with the help of an unknown spirit, had escaped, was enraged and not only banished the guards who were guarding the dragon to space but also immediately disposed of all the dinosaurs in his kingdom and also limited everybody in his kingdom from producing such large flying creatures again.

This pleased most of the humans because some tribes were starting to use the animals when attacking other tribes, and the tribes without such animals were quickly beaten. It did, unfortunately, deprive some tribes of food, as most of these animals could be captured for food and were not violent unless provoked by each other.

Lucifer was also upset that the humans kept forgetting him, so he decided to teach them a lesson they would never forget. So he created a huge drought, making the humans cry out for help to bring rain. No rain came; in fact, for months and months, Lucifer refused to grant rain, making the plains dry up into dust to make humans beg him for rain.

Lucifer had also made huge amounts of salt water; he made freshwater hard to find. As fresh water became harder and harder to get, the humans started to settle near fresh water and again started to worship Lucifer. To have their constant attention, Lucifer made the sun hotter and the rain scarcer so that everything became dry, and the plants eventually stopped growing.

More gods were invented, and more people worshiped Lucifer, which made him very happy. Lucifer quickly realized this was a wonderful way to control humans. When it became too good, plagues were sent to eat the crops and destroy most of what the humans had created. Again, Lucifer was happy, as these humans only thought about him when they were suffering, so he again made sure there was plenty of suffering so that the humans would pay attention to him.

Because of the relentless cruelty that had been produced by Lucifer, there were many spirits who were also very upset with Lucifer and who also wanted to cause him trouble. Some humans developed skills to bring some spirits back into the world, but the spirits were so upset that they would mostly only help if the act hurt or made Lucifer angry. Some spirits helped the humans but demanded a high price or made demands that only a few humans could actually achieve. This usually gave the spirits control of those humans, who would not get released till the demands agreed to had been met. The spirits inside the humans caused hatred and anger within them that they had no control over.

When the humans saw what was happening to these people, many times they tried to kill the human or lock them up in small rooms and feed them intermittently; in other cases, they let them starve to death, and the spirits within would then be banished to the controlling space created by Lucifer. Sometimes the spirits actually went and hid themselves before Lucifer could banish them to space, and in these cases, the spirits could roam around till they found another human host and remain there until the host human died.

In some cases, a few spirits who were roaming around could scheme by living in humans; they were able to give information and secrets to some humans who copied the information in writings. However, even after thousands of years, humans still had difficulty understanding them. Most of the information once found and not understood was destroyed or hidden for fear of being seen by others.

This attitude developed in many tribes and some hid the information, while others, not understanding, destroyed the information. Whatever the reason, some information that remained was put to the test or sold to others to try or destroyed. Some were able to get great advantages, while others, not understanding, fell victim to horrible deaths.

Over time, however, a large number of secret powers was slowly lost, and fewer and fewer people were able to create the power the original human users could produce.

ANGER

This pleased Lucifer, who thought with only his god creations, everyone would pay more attention to him; he kept busy creating ever so many that humans were again satisfied, and again for a time, Lucifer was happy.

Because of the humans' greed and desires, it became harder and harder for Lucifer to please all the humans, who were growing in large numbers, so Lucifer again created tribal fighting, which sometimes lasted for many years.

This had a small effect, but it was thought that larger numbers of humans should be culled. So Lucifer produced very powerful germs capable of mass destruction, which again pleased him because they again cried out his name and begged for help.

My storyteller now paused. With a frown, he asked, "Is anything about this story at this point familiar?"

I smiled and said, "It is similar but a little different to what we have been taught."

"He then said, "The next part, I feel, will totally confuse you, but this is what happened."

CHAPTER 7
CREATING EXTRA GODS

Earth was now at a very interesting phase; it had taken a few billion years (Earth's time) to reach this point in the story. So you can see I had to omit details so as to make the story easily understandable, as I do not have the time to fill in the exact happenings.

Lucifer had worked out that his very best and loyal spirits who worshiped him and did everything that was asked of them should be given extra rewards and, in some cases, extra powers to let the humans know that they were gods in their own right. Some were asked what kind of god they wanted to be, and others were assigned positions that Lucifer knew they would like. Every activity that happened on Earth was appointed a god. There were gods of the ocean, fire, water, wind, lightning, famine, crops, health, war, prosperity, and death, to name just a few that were created.

This pleased the humans, as they now had a god to ask for anything they wanted, which again pleased Lucifer, as when they called out to any of the gods, it was really Lucifer who told the god spirit to agree or to go back to sleep and wait till it received the approval to do it. Sometimes individual gods would decide to have some fun and deliberately cause trouble by sinking a ship or causing storms or strong winds to remind humans that they required help and that it was time to pay more attention.

Tribes had started to increase again, and even tribes previously unknown had started to grow and want more and more. This pleased Lucifer, as he was now being paid more attention to. The numbers grew and grew until Satan decided that another war was required. So he gave two rulers, one in the North and one in the South, the means to have a huge war and reduce the number of humans in the North and South.

He gave one a weapon called Capella's Glance, which is said to have been able to make a human disappear in a flash, and another a lightning bolt, which they say made elephant's skin turn white and made birds fall from the sky. Both these weapons were so powerful that both the Northern and Southern gods were able to eliminate each other's foes with great efficiency to a level where Lucifer was so pleased with the results that he made sure both weapons were completely destroyed, as he did not want his whole kingdom to be destroyed without his approval.

Thus, Lucifer banished the spirits that did not have his approval to special places that had been created for them and reminded the remaining leaders of the tribes to remember who was the most important god on Earth or else there would be another catastrophe that would never be forgotten.

Around this time, God wanted to bring a human back to find out exactly what was happening to most humans, so he reached down to a loyal believer and brought him directly up to the heaven without him dying on Earth. (I did not believe such a story was possible, but I checked Google and found this reference: Enoch, along with Noah, is one of Adam's most well-known descendants and is believed to be the author of the book of Enoch. He was also known as "Enoch, the scribe of judgment." Enoch was the son of Jared, the father of Methuselah and the great-grandfather of Noah.

He did not live quite as long as the other men, as he was taken by God when he was 365 years old, which makes him one of the only people whom God took to heaven without then dying. Courtesy Google (My only thought about this is that maybe Enoch was really a spirit in a human form, which would allow such an event to happen. I believe Jesus was the only other spirit to take a human form after his death and also return to heaven.)

CHAPTER 8
WARNING

Back in heaven, a meeting was called, and after a considerable amount of time, God told all the spirits what was happening on Earth. Questions were asked about possible solutions to help the humans on Earth. Some spirits were uncomfortable interfering, as they were happy in their worlds and wanted no part of helping. Others were happy with the idea of offering help to stop Lucifer from causing so much suffering. A vote was requested, and most of the other spirit kings agreed to help. But how to help? Because if they had to help, they had to take on a human form and be willing to be governed by the laws created by Lucifer on Earth.

"OK," said God, "let me consider what could be offered, and we will have another meeting when I have a solution." It seemed that only a few could enter the other world without being affected, so God asked the dragon and the phoenix, "Would you be prepared to enter Earth again and deliver a message to Lucifer and place several spells on the Earth and hide them well, before delivering the message?" Both agreed as they had become very good friends. God gave four packages to the dragon and also an additional power so that he could make multiple copies of himself to avoid capture, and to the phoenix, he gave extra powers to make up for the power she would lose upon entering Earth.

Off they went, and sometime later, they entered through the same gap that they'd escaped through earlier. Down they swooped. Many humans looked up, and some screamed in fear, while others thought another god had come to help, but most of the humans ran and hid, scared. The dragon went and hid the small packets containing the spells, while the phoenix kept others from looking at the dragon and later returned. Then both the phoenix and the dragon went to see Lucifer. Lucifer was outside his palace, and as he looked up with anger and surprise, both the phoenix and the dragon said, "We come in peace with a message from God, the ruler of all the universe."

As they landed, Lucifer summoned his black-power oracles, who surrounded both of them and wanted to capture the dragon but were very surprised to see a strange-looking bird, the likes of which they had never seen before.

"What is your message?" demanded Lucifer.

"We come in peace, but our Master and the God of the universe has a message that we think you should listen, as we must take an answer back to our God. It has reached his ears that you have used your power to demand that humans do as you ask or they will be made to suffer, and eventually you kill them and banish them to a specially prepared place you have created, where they stay until you decide if they can be let out, like a perpetual prison!"

"This is my world, and I can do as I like, so I do not need a lesser king who has no more power than me to say what I can and cannot do, so go and tell your pathetic god that he has no power here and to do as he pleases in his own kingdom. Also, tell him that if he dares to come here, I will challenge him here to see who is the most powerful god in the universe. If he comes and he wins, I will consider acknowledging him as the most powerful god.

Is there anything else?" Lucifer barked.

"Yes," said the dragon, "we have to also say that if you continue to act as you have over the last few hundred thousand years, you will experience a huge tragedy that will weaken your powers and cause you to never have the power you have now."

At that last comment, Lucifer started to laugh so hard that the ground shook, and all his guards also started to laugh, telling both the dragon and the phoenix to leave quickly or they would never be able to return because both would be locked up forever.

In parting, the dragon said, "There would be ten years of his kingdom's time to change or face retaliation for his actions."

Again, everybody burst into laughter and scorn, so, at that, both the dragon and the phoenix arose, again warning Lucifer not to be so hasty in his scorn. The dragon and the phoenix immediately left Lucifer's kingdom and quickly returned to heaven to report back to God. Both of them reported what Lucifer had said, who had no thought of considering the threat issued. They felt their visit would make Lucifer even worse just to show everyone he was king and god.

The dragon asked God, "Could I ask a question?"

"Yes."

"Why is it that all humans make it so important in measuring everything by time? We have no time, and it is not even a consideration, so why do they think the time is so important?"

"Well," replied God, "as Lucifer has made a limit as to the time a human can remain as a human before becoming a spirit again, they consider the word 'time' very important. Also, Lucifer has instilled a huge fear of dying, so all humans do not like the idea of dying. Because all past memories have been blocked, they have a fear of the unknown. This makes humans consider time as very important. It also gives Lucifer a huge power over humans."

"Thank you, my God," said the dragon.

Smiling, God again thanked his two faithful helpers for the help and for the news.

CHAPTER 9
THE GREAT FLOOD

Lucifer was still laughing about the visit from the dragon and the strange-looking bird when he remembered their message and started to think about what they may have actually come to say—that there would be trouble in ten years if he did not alter what he was doing? So he summoned all his armies, which were made up of every conceivable creature and of varied sizes, as well as his special black spirits, to look throughout his kingdom and look for anything that could hold or be a special curse, which may have been left by his visitors. "What would it look like?" they asked Lucifer.

"Maybe a gold box, a package that looks like it did not come from this world but would usually be warped with a gold rope. If anyone can find such a package, the person who finds it can have five wishes of anything they want as a reward." Immediately word was dispatched throughout the earth, asking everyone in the kingdom to look for anything that looked like it came from another world. They were to report immediately should anything be found that looked strange. Many humans, hearing about the amazing reward, also started looking high and low for the box or package. Some came forward with found boxes and others with carpets rolled up, but as hard as they looked, no one could find any packet left by anyone throughout the four corners of the kingdom.

After some time Lucifer decided it was a trick and that, in fact, nothing was left and that he should go back to what made him happiest, and that was making the humans think about him more. So he again made the tribes fight and invented new gods, and the more they killed and caused complete misery, the happier Lucifer was. In fact, he so much liked it, there were few humans in his kingdom who were not either trying to kill each other or making sure others could not harm them.

It seemed a very short time, that the time given by God had arrived, and Lucifer called his army together to say it was obvious that the message from that impostor God had no power, and that, in fact, he may even decide to attack this impostor's kingdom to teach him a lesson as to who was the greatest god. All of them agreeing seemed to make Lucifer happy, so he dispatched a couple of his black spirits to visit heaven to see how strong this so-called God was.

The black spirits were gone only for a very short time; they returned and told it was well guarded. In fact, there was only one entrance, so getting inside was all but impossible. Also, they explained that any spirit entering could never leave without the personal permission of God.

"How did you discover this so quickly?" bellowed Lucifer.

"At the gates were two of the largest dragons ever created, and although they were very fierce, they also answered any questions, and as long as they did not feel threatened, they were happy answering whatever questions we asked."

Hearing this Lucifer decided to do more planning, and pleased with the black spirits' results, he gave each a special wish.

Lucifer decided that the claim from that impostor God was not going to cause any problems, as it was past the deadline given to him, and although the high mountain volcanoes had stopped blowing smoke, Lucifer considered it a good sign and continued making the humans suffer even more. The land was dry, and clouds began to form to help the humans. Lucifer decided to allow them for a short while and paid little attention to them. It began to rain softly at first, and then it became a heavy storm, building in power with high winds and heavy rain. The ocean water was churned into high waves, which crashed into the land with huge force. As the days became weeks, the rain continued to fall in ever greater amounts, making it hard for humans to see or even walk outside.

Lucifer demanded the storms be stopped, and the more he demanded, the harder the rain came down. The humans were crying out for help, and again Lucifer commanded the rain to stop, but the rain came down harder. Some tribes moved to higher grounds, and some went to the tops of mountains, while others died before they could escape.

The rain continued, and still, the winds blew, and trees crashed to the ground, unable to withstand the force of the huge winds. The winds became stronger and stronger. Each time Lucifer demanded they stop, the harder they blew. The salt water churned and pounded against the land, growing in size over thirty meters and sometimes up to forty meters, crashing onto the land and taking all with it as the waters retreated into their reservoir. This continued for a long time, and the level of salt water rose up to cover most of Lucifer's kingdom. Most of his tribes had been destroyed, and the few lefts had spread thin throughout his kingdom. Most were frightened and lost, not caring about anything, except staying warm and giving no thought to any king or god. Eventually, the rains stopped, and the sun started to shine throughout the kingdom.

Lucifer knew this was the doing of this God from heaven but could not actually prove the situation. However, he decided to take revenge, which would make that God feel he had lost the power and make him sad and sorry for even trying to hurt him.

CHAPTER 10
THE CLEANUP

Lucifer decided he would not be beaten so quickly, and surveying his kingdom, he found that most of it was, in fact, under salt water, along with everything created, and there was little room for any humans to grow large.

So he commanded the mountains to rise and sink, allowing the water to move back to where it was supposed to be. He allowed the land to move and separate to make room for the water to recede and allow the land to see the sun and be able to be used by the humans again so that they would pay attention to him again. He made it such that the land could be moved in the future; in case a similar thing should occur, he could move things quickly to beat such a move from outside powers. What he did not consider was that by moving the mountains, a large amount of water was able to seep down to the center of the kingdom that quickly turned to steam, causing huge power vacuums, which put huge pressure inside his kingdom's base. This buildup of pressure opened cracks, allowing molten rock to pour over the land and lifting much of the land higher, even making large plains capable of supporting large populations for more humans.

Lucifer immediately started to create more spirits as humans, but this time he placed each tribe in a different part of his kingdom, with little or no contact with each other. In addition, he created a new language for each tribe, making it harder for the tribes to plot against him.

Again, they were happy with the new gods Lucifer provided. When each tribe became large, it pleased him even more. When there were fights and arguments, it made Lucifer even happier. He said to himself, "You stupid God, you helped me and did not hurt me, but I will plan revenge against you and your stupid kingdom."

Some of the spirits Lucifer created had small but interesting powers, able to create different animals but limited in size. The largest was an animal known as an elephant, which is still around in current times. Other animals were made for freshwater streams and the salt water; others were made for land, suitable for eating, and some were made as pets, although some pets that could not be controlled, in some cases, turned on their human keepers, eating them or just running away from their control.

My storyteller stopped and said, "I see that you are confused. Don't forget. I am not putting my story in a time frame, as time has no meaning to spirits!"

"Please continue," I replied.

THE CLEANUP

The kingdom became again alive with tribes growing and the humans were happy, being able to make other humans again. The only difference this time was that many tribes spoke a different language, and trading or mixing became a huge problem. Some decided to conquer other tribes and demand they learn their language or be killed. This pleased Lucifer, who encouraged such action.

Many tribes were kept in one place because they could not travel over what appeared to be huge lakes. So they stayed where they were and did not try to move from their areas. Some tribes made small wooden boats and tried to go to other places, which mostly sank, or they died of hunger and thirst. This made the humans think that the earth was flat and that they should never venture out of sight of the land.

At the start, after the great flood, small tribes survived, but larger groups had huge problems, because the trees and plants did not grow very well, and the animals available, although created by some spirits, quite often were eaten or, in many cases, because of lack of food moved to other areas. This caused hardship and limited the number of humans from multiplying, which satisfied Lucifer for a short time.

As rain fell and washed the salt deeper into the ground, plants started to grow, and slowly some animals returned. Again, humans started to increase in numbers and forgot about Lucifer. This again made Lucifer create some new gods to satisfy the humans, who liked the gods very much and many times used the gods created to excuse their failings or blame for misfortune.

Lucifer also realized that humans needed help, so he created humans with varied abilities to make sure the humans always had something to make them try harder. Some were gifted in making items suitable to use to make their lives more comfortable, and others had skills to make new inventions for hunting, but Lucifer also knew that items used for hunting could also be used to fight and destroy other humans, which pleased him very much. Some actually had other abilities, such as flying or moving over the world very fast, so they could report all news to Lucifer, which allowed him to plan and make new ways for humans to fight or want larger areas for their tribes.

Some animals were created to assist in covering huge areas or were made to guard certain areas that Lucifer wanted humans to be kept away from. The humans were content, and over the next one hundred thousand years, they had very few problems, except that many now we're starting to get larger populations, and some started to explore new areas, and many were surprised to encounter other humans, whom they could not understand, but seeing better ideas and better abilities among them, they quickly returned to their own people to tell about it. Lucifer now decided it was time to plan revenge against that annoying God, in that place called heaven, for the damage he had caused in his kingdom. So calling his guards to come together, he started to plan revenge for what had happened to his kingdom!

CHAPTER 11
WORD ARRIVED

Back in heaven, God had been getting progressive reports as to what had been happening on Earth and was not surprised to get word that Lucifer was planning revenge in return for what had transpired in his kingdom. God summoned all the spirits of the spirit world and again explained that Lucifer was planning a revenge attack and that all spirits should be aware that a war could develop and that they should all be alert to any activity that could upset the calm of the spirit world. He also pointed out that Lucifer had strong powers and may try to convince others to join him in his attempt to get revenge against heaven. All agreed to make sure that their kingdoms were on alert and that God need not have to worry about any spirits outside Earth assisting this very bad spirit ruling Earth. God saw his faithful dragons guarding the front gates and gave them special powers to be able to stop any attacks from Earth so that should they detect any threat, they'd have the authority and power to defend themselves, the kingdom of heaven and the faithful spirits in heaven. He also strengthened his kingdom against any possible evil by making a barrier around it, such that no power or spirit could breach it.

God was also informed that because of the changes made on Earth now no spirit could enter Earth without now taking on a human form and that any spirit who entered Earth could not keep its magic powers but would be subjected to the laws and powers of Earth. He listened and was worried that this new change would limit any help to the humans who were now bound to Earth.

So he decided to work out a solution and said that he would need time to decide what and if any help could be given in the future, especially should Lucifer decide to attack or cause trouble in the spirit world. He also knew that once a spirit turned into a human form, it was given a fear of death and no previous knowledge that it previously had as a spirit was retained, and this worried him as to how he could counter this strange condition made for the humans, but he also saw the extra power it gave Lucifer over his kingdom. He now also knew that when a human died, the spirit could not leave Earth without being given permission by Lucifer, which made it difficult to come up with a plan to help. God even knew now that any spirit who did not please Lucifer was sent to a special place, where it could not escape and could not become a human again without Lucifer's approval.

How was he to send a spirit to Earth, have it transform into a human, yet lose all knowledge as to why it was actually in this strange kingdom? God made it known that he needed time to solve this problem but also that he was sure a solution could be found.

CHAPTER 12

REVENGE FROM EARTH

Meanwhile, Lucifer had decided he would attack the strongest points of heaven and give a message to that pompous God that indeed he was not the most powerful god and that he should be very careful as to what he tried to do in future to Earth. Knowing that heaven was guarded by two dragons that had huge powers, Lucifer created a most beautiful dragon, with all the powers of deception that a spirit could possess. This dragon was instructed to approach the dragons stationed at heaven's gates and make the dragons want to be with her and to tease them both till they both desired her and then suggest that if they were to combat each other, the winner could have her.

At first, each dragon, not fearing a female dragon, played and swooped around in space in fun. Completely forgetting their duties, as it had been so long since either had seen a female dragon, both of them wanted her. As they flew around playing, both very happy to be able to see another dragon, they forgot what they were supposed to do and only concentrated on chasing their prey. They became less and less worried about guarding the gates. Soon the female dragon tricked one into believing that she was fond of him and secretly kidded the other to try harder to win her affection. Soon both the dragons began to fight over the female dragon. As she watched, for the first time there seemed to be a conflict in the kingdom. She happily continued to tease them to trigger a conflict between them, as was planned by her master.

Sure enough, both the dragons soon started to quarrel and fight as to who had the rights to the beautiful female dragon! After some time, the larger of the two dragons turned on the smaller, and blowing his greatest fire, he burned the smaller dragon along its back, rendering him unable to fly, and the smaller dragon crawled back to the gates that he should have been guarding.

The larger dragon then went to get his prize, and to his surprise, the female dragon immediately spun around and headed straight back to Earth. Not realizing the direction she had gone in, the larger dragon pursued his prey at great speed through space, with only one thing in his mind—he had to have his beautiful dragon. Down to Earth, she went, with the male dragon in hot pursuit, and it was not until he had entered Earth that he realized that all his power and speed had vanished. Realizing that he had been completely tricked, the dragon went into hiding, knowing he could not return and that God would be very mad at his stupid actions.

His prize also vanished; she headed directly to Lucifer to report a successful venture and to tell him where the other dragon was hiding. Lucifer was very happy with the female dragon's performance, and he gave her several wishes. Leaving her to her desires, he went to plan his next move against God, whom he had come to dislike so much.

CHAPTER 13

ANGER IN THE HEAVENS

God, on hearing that his dragons had been tricked, flew into a rage, and headed for the gates to ask the smaller dragon what had happened that his kingdom was now threatened and nothing had been done about it! Seeing his smaller dragon in extreme pain and unable to fly, he felt sorry and immediately cured his pain and then asked what happened. The smaller dragon explained, "The most beautiful dragon we had ever seen came by to play, and both of us were lost in its beauty. Unable to reason, we both followed her, and it caused a fight, in which the bigger dragon won."

Then God immediately decided that henceforth dragons would not be guarding his kingdom from outside but from within, where no other dragon could ever trick them. When asked what happened to the other dragon, God was told that he had followed the female dragon to Earth and had not returned and that it was thought that he must have followed her right into the earth's realm, from where he could not return, unless killed. God was furious that his kingdom had been tricked by such a cheap trick and decided not only to strengthen his kingdom but also to definitely find ways to help the humans trapped on Earth and show Lucifer who was the most powerful god in the universe. He called his most brave and wise spirits together to inform them of what happened and also to plan help and assistance for the dragon who was now trapped on Earth as well as a plan to try to help the humans there who had no idea what type of king was ruling them.

Everybody assembled, God asked for plans to visit Earth and how to get there and still be able to remember what they had to do and then carry out their tasks.

"This is a problem I want all of you to consider, and let's meet back here in a while to discuss what you have been able to devise to get to Earth and then return." A few asked, "What is the problem? Because we can get back by being killed, we can return here."

"Yes," said God, "but you will have a huge fear of death, and that will make it very difficult for you to realize your true purpose there, and so you will fight the idea of dying. Also, Lucifer has put a barrier that prevents spirits from leaving and, therefore at this time, any spirits who enter Earth are confined to Earth forever. Let's meet again after a bit and discuss your plans, but please do not take too long making plans."

CHAPTER 14
SEARCH FOR THE DRAGON

Lucifer knew that his plan to get one of the dragons away from that stupid heaven's gate into his kingdom had worked and he was very happy about it because he knew that if he could capture the dragon again, this time he could stay never to be released, which would cause God great anger. Immediately he sent his guards over the land searching for the dragon, knowing he would be found, and then he planned to make the dragon suffer for a great period of time.

The dragon had some extra powers, but they were limited when he entered Earth; he could still fly, and his power to blow fire was still OK, so he decided he would help the humans and try to limit Lucifer's ability to harm them. First, he circled the kingdom, scaring some and exciting some, but at each sighting, Lucifer became more and more upset, demanding the dragon be captured. Mostly the dragon hid during the day and ventured out at night, looking for ways to help the humans, but it was very difficult, as most of them ran away when they saw him.

However, when he encountered the servants of the king wherever possible, he burned them so they would be of little use to Lucifer, and that made Lucifer even more upset, to a point that he offered any wish to the ones who could tell Lucifer where this dragon was hiding. As the dragon flew around Lucifer's kingdom, he saw many things that surprised him. There were humans of different colors and many areas where the humans seemed very poor, with very little to make them happy. So, first, he decided to make precious metals and stones, which the humans would soon realize were valuable, to make them happy. So as he flew over the lands where he saw the suffering humans, he planted gold, silver, diamonds, emeralds, rubies, and many other precious stones in the ground. Some of the gold he put in easy-to-find places, and some he put in hard-to-find places, but it was enough to make the humans think of ways to make themselves happy. In some areas, he put only one or two metals or stones, but in the poorest areas, he placed enough to make everybody happy. In the North, he placed diamonds, gold, silver, rubies, and sapphires. In the South, he put diamonds, emeralds, silver, gold, and many lesser stones, which he knew the humans would like. He did not think that such riches would also cause the humans to fight and kill among themselves just to keep the riches between a few. Being a pure spirit, with only good intentions, he could not imagine the suffering it would cause to so many in later generations.

Also, he noticed that the humans in the southern areas seemed fearful of him, and some tried to kill him for the reward that had been offered by Lucifer. The only place he seemed sort of safe was in the northern areas, where many considered him a beautiful and powerful spirit; for them, he was a blessing and they considered themselves extremely lucky to just see him. By this time Lucifer was becoming furious that no one could find this annoying dragon, so he doubled the reward for anyone who could find and either capture the dragon or tell him where he was hiding.

The dragon knew everyone was looking for him, so he decided to make copies of himself, which would act as decoys should anyone actually get too close to where he was hiding. This trick worked very well, because all of a sudden, the king was being told that the dragon was here or in the north or in the south all at the same time. It even started to seem to Lucifer that there actually was no dragon and that it simply was the imagination of humans wanting a reward for nothing.

Lucifer called off the hunt, and all the kingdom settled down, not caring about whether the dragon was real or just a story for children. However, again Lucifer heard stories of a dragon that was helping some and even protecting some. This angered him, so he sent his guards out to look for this dragon to see if it was real or just imagination or just stories based on nothing but greed.

The dragon hid in the day inside a huge mountain, which had access through a tunnel via the sea in a high northern country. So good was the hiding place that no human could ever see him enter or leave even if they knew the inside of the mountain very well. The cave was covered in bright sparkling stones, which gave an eerie look, and it was not completely dark, as the light came in through the cracks in the mountain but which could not be easily seen.

During the day, the dragon stayed inside and at night it flew over the kingdom, looking for ways to help humans without being caught. Sometimes a gift was left—a piece of gold or silver or a precious stone. The humans began to say, "The dragon is lucky. No one should help Lucifer in finding this dragon." But the time was passing very fast, and the dragon still had to find a way out from this kingdom. It also happened that several of the decoy dragons that he had created had been killed, as the decoys had no magic powers and could not fight greater powers; they were easy prey for the demons sent to find them.

Back in heaven, God was very worried about his dragon even though he had acted very foolishly, but the dislike for Lucifer was enough to grant forgiveness to the dragon should he ever return. Again, he asked the phoenix for help in finding the dragon and inform him that he was forgiven and could return to heaven and remain in heaven if he could get back.

SEARCH FOR THE DRAGON

After lengthy discussions, the phoenix departed again in search of her faithful friend, the dragon. Again, she approached the same place where she entered the last time and swooped down to find him. Making herself invisible, she flew high and low, looking and calling their secret call to see if the dragon could hear, but there was no answer. Even after many weeks of flying across the four corners of this kingdom, she could not find any trace, and although very tired, she was convinced the dragon was in this kingdom. Maybe in the North, she thought as she soared high above, calling as loud as she could, but there was still no answer. In her desperation, she thought she had to go down and ask if the dragon had been seen anywhere, so swooping down and changing into a human form, she approached a person and asked, "Have you seen or heard about a large dragon recently?"

He said, "Yes, I have, but I am sure it was attacked and killed by the king's guards."

Curious, she asked, "How long ago?"

"We do not know, but some time ago, we heard a dragon was killed, and the king held a celebration to mark the event." The phoenix was shattered, and it took all of her strength to say "Thank you for the information" as she moved away, hiding huge tears as they ran down her face. Moving out of sight, she changed back and flew as high as she could to try to understand what she had just been told. Part of her said, "Impossible," and the other half kept asking, "How and why?" Looking around, she searched for the tallest tree to hide in and gather her thoughts. Finding one, she landed on the highest tip and broke down into uncontrollable tears and sadness. She cried so much that it felt as if rain was falling all around the tree, and she felt so overcome with sadness that she just wanted to give up and return to heaven.

Something made her stop and look around, as she thought she could sense something, but she did not know what. Yes, she thought, I feel the dragon, and I am sure he is not dead, but if he is not, what dragon did Lucifer kill? This again brought huge tears to her eyes as she started to cry again. A fierce wind started to blow, and her resting place started to sway back and forth until she was forced to go down to the lower branches. Being so tired, she drifted off to sleep, with tears still running down her cheeks.

While asleep, she had a dream: she and the dragon were flying together over the hills across the blue sky, laughing and very happy together. They both flew high then swooped down, racing each other to see who could fly faster. The dragon won the race, and just as she was challenging him for a second race, she awoke with a start. Not knowing what woke her, she flew straight up to see what could have disturbed her from such a high tree.

Nothing was there. Just the empty sky. So very disappointed, she returned to the tree but was not comfortable. Again, she started to think about the dragon. Could he be alive? Confused, she relaxed and started to drift into a half-asleep, half-awake condition, when again she awoke with a start, feeling something had reminded her of the dragon. Could it be right? she thought and flew high into the night sky to again see if her feelings were right.

As she looked around, she saw a huge splash in the sea, which she could not help but wonder if it was the dragon. Flying over to where she thought the splash was, she looked down but could see nothing. What could make such a splash? she thought and decided to remain close by to see if there was another splash in the same position. She watched all night, and nothing splashed, and nothing she could see gave any indication that the dragon could be anywhere, but something made her wait and watch. She watched all day. Not even a fish splashed in the water; there was nothing. She started to consider going elsewhere to look when again there was a huge waterspout as if something was rushing out of the water at a huge speed.

Then she saw the dragon speeding toward the sky, leaving a spray of water behind. At first, she was in such a shock that she just froze, and then she sprang to life and sped at her fastest speed after her great friend. Soon she was on his tail, screaming, "Stop! It's me! Dragon, stop!"

Then with disbelief, the dragon stopped and swung around as if struck by lightning. "What? How? Wow! the dragon exclaimed as he was so pleased to see his great friend, the phoenix.

"We must talk," said the phoenix. "Let's go down and talk; it is so important!"

The dragon was very happy and immediately swooped down into a huge forest, with the phoenix right behind. Both of them were so happy to see each other that they started talking at the same time before realizing that they had not heard what the other had said. The phoenix said, "God has forgiven you, and it would be wonderful if you could leave with me and return safely to heaven." The dragon replied, "Indeed, I have been very stupid, and also I feel extremely sorry for the humans under Lucifer so I have decided to stay here and help as much as I can until God also finds a way to help them.

Then I will come back if I can. But the other problem is that I now cannot return in my current form, as I have been changed into the same condition as humans and cannot leave unless I die. With so much to do, it is better if I stay and help until the day comes when I can gladly return, and it will only be a short time, as humans only live about a hundred years in this kingdom's time.

Maybe I can survive a hundred years and, if lucky, also help the humans for a longer period of time." Then the dragon asked the phoenix if she could return. She said, "Yes, because, for some strange reason, the transformation that changes all spirits into a human-like condition here did not have that effect on me. So yes, I can return with messages or information if required." But she was so happy to see the dragon that she wanted to stay a while with him before she returned.

The dragon explained that Lucifer had made more changes, which made it even harder for any help to be given from heaven. "What has been changed?" asked the phoenix, showing great concern.

"Well," the dragon said, "Lucifer has made it even harder for the spirits to leave and has made a space underground, where all spirits must go to when their bodies die. They have a choice to become another human but only to serve Lucifer. But they can only go around in a circle at Lucifer's decision. This has made it impossible to leave this place and has basically confined all spirits to this world. They are unable to leave and must do what Lucifer demands, or they will remain in the space below without any hope of being saved. This change has made the spirits very sad, as they feel they will be trapped here forever unable to leave this world and having to serve Lucifer forever."

This news shocked the phoenix, who suggested she should maybe get back to heaven and explain these new changes and ask God if anything could be done to help the spirits captured in this everlasting cage. The dragon also suggested that although he was not sure it could be possible that when he eventually also died, he may also be captured as a spirit and kept in the cave with the other spirits, never able to return to heaven.

The phoenix was distraught at the thought of the dragon never being able to return, and although she wanted to stay with him, she suggested that she should get back to heaven as soon as possible and explain all this to God. The dragon wanted to continue talking with the phoenix, but he was aware that something huge had to happen if the spirits under Lucifer were to be saved, and so he asked the phoenix to return and explain the situation to God as soon as she could. He also asked if she could tell God that he was so sorry for the wrong he'd done and the stupid action that resulted in him being tricked. Wishing the dragon a safe stay and promising to ask God to fix the problem and the unhappiness that Lucifer had created in this world. With tears streaming down her face, she flew up to the top, and finding the small gap through which she entered, she flew as fast as she could back to heaven.

CHAPTER 15
PHOENIX'S RETURN TO HEAVEN

On returning to heaven, the phoenix immediately went to God and explained in great detail what was happening on Earth and asked if there was anything he could do to help destroy the powers of Lucifer. God explained that although it was very tempting to interfere and destroy Lucifer, it was totally impossible, because the laws were if a spirit were to kill another, then both the spirits would be destroyed. So such a request was not possible, but maybe they could arrange a bridge for the spirits trapped on Earth to escape, but that also had problems, because the barriers created by Lucifer prevented the spirits from leaving.

"What should we do then?" asked the phoenix. "I need some time to examine the position and also time to decide how to punish Lucifer for his actions. So please go and rest, and inform our other dragon about his trapped friend and help him understand the position on Earth so that he knows that it is important not to be tricked in the future. Also, advise him to be even more alert to the schemes Lucifer might hatch to try to hurt our heaven."

Then God again summoned all the spirits for a meeting and explained the basic problems developing on Earth. He also asked for ideas to help any spirits who did manage to escape to be able to find heaven.

Several spirits suggested, "Could a council be formed of all the spirits with the knowledge of war and defense so that all options could be suggested and a plan be prepared to present to God for a final decision?" So a council was formed, made up from the most powerful and the smartest spirits, to come up with a plan to save the spirits from Earth. The whole story of Earth was explained—about the dragon being tricked and a barrier being set in place to prevent spirits from leaving and how the spirits could not enter Earth without taking on a human form, which eliminated all memory as to why they were there in the first place. History was also shown about the cruel way Lucifer controlled the humans and forced them to be captive spirits when they died, as they did not know how to get out, and even if they did, they would have no knowledge of the beautiful heaven. The huge possible threat to heaven, the demands from Earth, and the challenges made by Lucifer to God were also aired.

The council had one aim: to punish Lucifer and take away his power so that he could not trap spirits from leaving if they wanted to ever again.

CHAPTER 16
A SOLUTION IS PRESENTED

Many ideas were discussed, and some ideas were to give some spirits the power to fly faster than any other spirits and to guide any spirits who escaped from Earth back to heaven. But it was pointed out that spirits could not escape and that because they did not know heaven existed they had no reason to escape. Also, the only possible way out was blocked to prevent any spirit from leaving, so whoever went to Earth would also be prevented from leaving.

Others suggested that God help humans without going to Earth by sending thoughts or dreams to selected humans so they could understand and make plans to escape. Some spirits mentioned the great floods that God had sent to the earth, so why not send floods to destroy the bad humans? But again it was pointed out that good humans would also be killed, and they would still have no knowledge about heaven. Also, it was mentioned that once a human did die, Lucifer merely assigned them another human form to continue his work. They continued to discuss the problem, and although many had short-term solutions, it was agreed that one solution alone was not going to work and that maybe many plans had to be tried together to achieve the best results. It was decided to contact God and see if his wisdom could improve any of the ideas suggested.

When God was given the many options without any plan, he decided to take all the ideas and carefully try to find a solution and gave instructions that a further meeting would be called, where all would hear his decisions. Sometime later God called a meeting to show how he'd decided to fix the problems on Earth. He pointed out that humans were born in the womb of a woman, and he had found a way to send thoughts and messages to carefully selected humans, which he said could guide them, and even though it might take a long time, once they understood, it would accomplish what he wanted to be done. He also explained that once he had sent the power for them to understand and informed them who he was, he could actually talk with them at times, which he hoped would guide them to let other humans understand that there was a heaven and that he would be happy to receive them all. This plan sounded really good, so all the spirits agreed God should start immediately to set his ideas in motion, and all agreed that their God was the greatest in the universe.

CHAPTER 17

SOWING THE SEEDS

The initial idea was well received in heaven; all the spirits were happy that a solution was, at last, being put into place to take power away from Lucifer and save the many captive spirits who had no idea about heaven; in fact, it now seemed possible that they could all escape from Earth and come to heaven. Slowly people were chosen by God, and he watched from a distance to see if his plan would work.

What he did not count on was Lucifer had somehow discovered that certain spirits were in some ways beginning to be in conflict with his demands and ideas. So he started to find ways to make sure the few spirits who had ideas that appeared to be against him and his plans would be given choices they could not refuse and so counter the ideas planted by God in them and thus ensure that they forgot God's ideas and only desired to praise Lucifer. This frustrated God to a point he became quite upset, as a lot of effort and time had been used to put this plan into action.

God had sent loud messages to the spirits he'd given power to, but again many fell to other temptations and quickly lost the desire to continue listening to God's thoughts. In fact, many, when presented with temptations, not only forgot about God but also actually acted against any ideas that would in any way help God.

Some achieved high ranks in armies and even in running their own businesses. They became powerful above most other humans, and the desire to have wealth and power was much greater than a promise from God that they could not see. In fact, it seemed no matter how many were chosen, all became masters to Lucifer, and once power was achieved, they only had thoughts and desires for Lucifer. Again God called a meeting of the spirits and explained that Lucifer was winning the conflict, as the desire for gold was far greater than a place in heaven, which most could not understand. So he again asked the spirits to discuss the problems and come back with a possible plan that may work.

Looking down at Earth and looking at the humans who controlled the power and all who were slaves working for other humans, an idea was considered, which seemed to have the ability to achieve what God wanted. There was a race whose scriptures described the arriving of the most powerful god, who would allow them to control the earth; they would be free from many years of slavery and, in fact, could later control everybody on Earth.

God had established small tribes of humans who'd kept a low profile and believed God would come from heaven and deliver the kingdom to them. This, in fact, was one of the reasons that more powerful humans could enslave them because they were not skilled in war but skilled in writing and studying the scriptures, and all believed in a savior who would give their people freedom from slavery and grant everlasting life.

CHAPTER 18

IMPLEMENTATION OF PLAN SAVIOR

The spirits were again called together, and it was explained that certain human tribes had kept and still believed there was, in fact, one God, but they had been enslaved and kept under control as slaves to very powerful humans, and God decided he would use these tribes to defeat Lucifer. He explained he had to first test some of the tribes to make sure that they would be loyal no matter what risk was involved, and if they passed the tests, he would make sure that rewards were given to the tribes who kept to his teachings.

"How will you achieve this idea if you cannot enter Earth but only send voices or visions to give your messages?" "At this time I have to see if it is possible to guide the loyal tribes out of the demands of Lucifer, and should this not work, I have another plan, but it is a last-chance

IMPLEMENTATION OF PLAN SAVIOR

plan, so I do not want to discuss it at this time." So arrangements were made to send messages and signs to certain tribes to see if they would pledge loyalty to God.

Here my storyteller stopped and explained that there were many stories written in the scriptures explaining the tests and visions that were given to the chosen tribes. So to explain each would only waste time, which we did not have in an unlimited way, so he passed over the known information.

Suffice to say that the tribes were promised to be led out of slavery and taken to a new land, which they would be able to call their own, and all they had to do was to continue to recognize the God in heaven as the one and only true God. A man was chosen to lead them out of slavery, and he did lead them for many years over the deserts, looking for their home. Although the food was, at times, provided to them, many among them became unhappy and even resentful of their leader. Many complained that slavery was probably better than running around the desert with no actual destination except a blind promise.

It was pointed out that believing and accepting God was the first rule to being accepted and being able to receive the blessings promised. Again, many were unhappy, asking when would all this happen and when would they be shown their promised land. They were assured it would be as soon as a message would be given with instructions about the promised land and to be patient. A short time later, their leader called all of them together and said he had to go to a mountain to get the message and that the people should be calm and wait for his return.

The story is well known, as when their leader returned after some time, the people had made their own god from the gold and silver that the tribes had with them to the horror, anger, and frustration of their leader. The gold was destroyed, and abuse and condemnation were leveled at the perpetrators who had allowed such a thing to transpire.

He explained that he had been given a holy set of rules, which the tribes had to live by when they arrived at their promised land. Many wanted to see what the rules were and immediately became upset that such basic ideas actually went directly against what they were taught and so the tribes began to split.

Some agreed nonviolence was a good idea, while others pointed out that they could not control the world as promised if they were not allowed to fight for it. How could any tribe punish the wrongdoers if they could not exact similar vengeance as was done against them? They felt, in fact, that such actions would surely lead them back to being slaves! Sometime later they arrived at the promised land, and again many who expected huge castles and gold-paved roads were totally disappointed when all they saw was hills and stony mountains. "We have walked for over thirty years, and you show us land with stones and rocks, and you call this the promised land?" they exclaimed. After many arguments, it was agreed

IMPLEMENTATION OF PLAN SAVIOR

that to fight among themselves was wrong and that the sooner they started to build what was needed, the happier all would be. During this time God was watching what was happening and became angry that humans could so easily forget his ideas and only desire riches and power.

Lucifer had sowed many seeds into all his subjects, which included personal desires, and once considered even in the smallest degree, they would grow and develop into very strong desires that only a few people could tame. Even the leaders and holy men suffered the same demand for personal desires, and Lucifer knew this was a way he could defeat God so that none of his subjects would even want to know or listen to such boring ideas as put forward by God or by his prophets or his teachings.

God realized that this was becoming a problem and wondered if there was any way he could get his message across to the humans that they were being tricked and held captive for the express pleasure of Lucifer. So angels and signs were sent along with other humans who were known as prophets, who again warned the humans that they should take care and follow the teachings of God and that there was another kingdom they should try to understand.

This seemed to work for very short periods, as the humans looked at the ideas and agreed that they were very fine but also quickly forgot about them, as the ideas seemed too far fetched and did not fit with what they wanted here and now. Being angered that the humans could say one thing today and the next day consider other ideas, promise today and forget tomorrow, God decided that the only way to confirm the humans really understood his message was to give tests to chosen humans, which would confirm they understood and were willing no matter the challenge to obey the commands.

This, of course, was accepted by the humans who were given the tests, but other humans again questioned it: What power could test so hard and give so little or, worse, no actual rewards other than a promise sometime in the future when they died?

CHAPTER 19

MORE GODS TO CONSIDER

During this time Lucifer realized that somehow God could send ideas and messages to some chosen humans, and by the time Lucifer realized that messages or signs had been sent, it was too late. So Lucifer decided that if he created other gods for the humans, it would make it even harder for God to achieve anything, as humans could be easily confused, and again he would not only win but would also make the messages from God seem very distant. Many gods were added to his list, some claiming to grant great wealth, some offering fertility, and some offering victory in war. In fact, humans liked these gods as they met their immediate needs, and again, for a while, Lucifer gained more followers and was happy that he was winning.

Lucifer also added a clever touch, he had created most humans with desires and wishes they wanted, and when it was explained that the new gods promised a return to Earth if all was not achieved by them in this life, they were happy. They were promised that after many returns, they could actually sit with God on the highest plain. So no matter what their position in this life, they could achieve better the next time around.

Many humans loved this new idea, as they also were offered the chance of riches and power, which they could achieve in time, provided they worshiped this or that god; thus, they were won over. This idea also established a set desire that the only heaven was here and that all they had to do was wait, and all riches they desired would be provided. This also gave the spirits the understanding and belief that they should stay in this world no matter what others said.

Lucifer was very happy, as his gods offered more hope to humans, and the teachings were given to each god also catered to the short-term desires of humans. More and more ideas were introduced, and the humans took and embraced these new gods and their ideas enthusiastically.

Of course, these gods were the makings of Lucifer, so empty promises and assurances meant nothing, as the humans could do nothing to hurt Lucifer. By the time they realized it was not as promised, it would be too late, and they just went into Lucifer's holding pen, unable to get out and with one choice: worship Lucifer or just stay there forever. During this time Lucifer became aware that God was trying to destroy his power, but because he also had huge powers, he was able to stop God from causing trouble. God's interference was actually helping Lucifer because it gave him reasons to strengthen his world and make any attack by God nearly impossible, as force could not be used to win this battle.

It was a battle for the souls and not physical or monetary gains. Lucifer knew this, so all he had to do was cater to the selfish desires he had given humans, and for sure he would win. The fact that spirits could not be destroyed without the destruction of both the souls ensured that no spirits could be destroyed in Lucifer's domain. This made him very confident that he could defeat God in any confrontation started by him and laughed at the simple attacks that were being tried by him.

God had been watching what was happening and decided he could beat Lucifer with his own plan of offering riches and power to the humans who followed his teachings. He set in motion a plan, which would see many of the tribes who were led into the promised land be given chances to achieve many of their desires if they followed the teachings of God.

God thought that only riches and power would achieve his goals, but this plan fed directly into Lucifer's lap. Some were given choices of what they wanted, and others were given tests to check if they were worthy of such a task, but sadly all were tested quietly by Lucifer first, who by this time discovered ways to find out who these chosen humans were.

He instilled desires knowing each one's weakness, and in most cases, he was able to win the game started by God. Some became powerful kings themselves, showing such great wisdom that only few could match them even today. Others became powerful generals and officials, but all went the same way, as all fell to the temptations shown and offered by Lucifer. It was only at death or when their power was gone that they realized what a huge mistake they had made, but sadly, by then it was too late.

God called everybody to a serious meeting to make a new plan to beat Lucifer and help the trapped humans. The meeting went on for a long time, with most saying to isolate Lucifer. God was, by this time, becoming very upset, so again the spirits suggested to forget him, but God said, "No, we must try to save the trapped souls in this very bad kingdom."

Many of the attendees pointed out that the only way was to actually go there and confront Lucifer, but there was possibly only one spirit with the power to beat Lucifer, and that was God or his Son.

CHAPTER 20

A NEW PLAN

Again, Lucifer laughed and showed God that he was, in fact, the ruler of this part of the universe and that God could not win in this fight. God was, by this time, becoming very upset, so again he called everybody for a serious meeting to make a new plan to beat Lucifer and help the trapped humans. The meeting went on for a long time, with most saying to isolate Lucifer and forget him, but God said, "No, we must try to save the trapped souls in this very bad kingdom." Many of the attendees pointed out that the only way was to actually go there and confront Lucifer, but there was possibly only one spirit with the power to beat Lucifer, and that was God or his Son.

At first, God would not entertain any such idea presented, but after much time discussing other ideas, each time it came back to these two main ideas, that either God or his Son would have to enter Earth's domain and defeat Lucifer. So very elaborate plans were made, and after many discussions with his Son on the risks and problems he would maybe have to encounter in Lucifer's domain, his Son agreed to go on such a journey to help all the souls trapped in this very bad kingdom. It was then discovered that the only way he could enter this area and still be able to confront Lucifer and defeat him was to enter Earth like all other humans and be born in the same way. Again the dangers of possible loss of complete communication or even the actual reason for his visit were then pointed out to him.

He was told that his powers could be maintained at times, but because of the barriers established by Lucifer, it was possible that they could be interrupted at times. It was also explained that, in fact, he could even be reduced to human abilities, which could cloud his judgment and even make him forget his actual propose for being there. This made Lucifer very confident that he could defeat God in any confrontation started and laughed at the simple attacks that were being tried by him.

CHAPTER 21

THE ARRIVAL

Plans were made. First, a person had to be found without Lucifer's knowledge that the Son of God was going to be sent to his domain to defeat him and free the souls trapped there unable to leave for hundreds of thousands of years. It was also decided that it should be a very low-key event, which would not bring attention to Lucifer or his many spies who were always looking for attacks by God. After many years of looking, a person was chosen, who met all the conditions that would allow the transfer of God's Son.

God had established several messengers well in advance, which, for security reasons, he sent to be next to his Son when he was born. These people actually had eminent power, but they were instructed to remain as simple observers, and only in the event of danger to God's Son should they allow their position to be known. The event happened as planned, and God was very happy that although it was only the beginning, all was going as he planned.

His Son was born, and as instructed, his name was to be called Jesus. From his very beginning, he was able to understand his reason for being on Earth and quickly learned the ways of these humans. He was so clever compared to others that even as a very young person, many older people wanted to hear what he had to say. Many were drawn to him so strongly and so completely that nothing anyone could say could drag them away. His wisdom and understanding was such that even the scribes and holy men of the day were amazed at his understanding and ability to discuss even the most complex ideas, which had many asking who this young person was. By this time Lucifer had also gotten word that there was a boy with immense learning. He immediately went to see for himself and see if he could identify this amazing person. At the first look, he could not remember such a soul but decided to watch him and also make another barrier in case he was not from this world.

It was at this time that Jesus had trouble communicating with his Father, and he started to make sometimes irrational decisions, which made all realize he was, in fact, human and not some strange invader. God began to get very upset at this and increased the power to communicate with his Son. Again his Son returned to being very smart, and again Lucifer became interested in this amazingly clever person. So Lucifer now sent his own controlled spies to find out just who this person was and make him say openly in front of everyone who he was. When asked just who he was or who he thought he was, Jesus openly stated he was the "Son of God." This worked perfectly in favor of Lucifer, and again he baited Jesus to declare just who he was, and again he claimed he was the Son of the true God of the universe.

Now Lucifer realized who this person was and immediately started plans to destroy this challenge. First, his plan was to discredit Jesus among the people to show what a fraud he was and then to turn the people against him so that people would complete the work and send this Jesus back to where he had come from or, better still, try to keep him captive just to annoy God. This would also show God just who was the most powerful god in the universe.

The message that Jesus was trying to deliver was peace and kindness, which was the exact opposite of what was being taught by Lucifer. Lucifer was only interested in conflict, and he wanted wars, hatred, jealousy, fornication, murder, and every other wrong to be established in his kingdom, and anyone who wanted other changes was considered as an enemy to be destroyed.

The universe that Jesus had come from had no wars or conflict or anger or anything like that was established in this world, so it was a huge shock when Jesus realized what huge differences and what huge challenges had to be overcome for him to win. Messages from heaven were not constant, and his ability to ask for help was only available at times, but there were long gaps when

WATER AND OIL

no communication was available similar to how communications get interrupted today. So trying to show people who had been taught wrongly or demonstrating that a kind word achieved more than a curse or a fight was very difficult.

There was no television or radio, and only a few could understand writing. Also, of course, no Internet was there as is the case today, so messages, no matter how powerful at the time, were only heard by a few people. Lucifer sent his messengers time and again to try to get Jesus to curse or to make mistakes, and yes, as he was human, he did make some mistakes, and he did lose his temper, but after he realized his mistakes, he tried to change, but it was too late. His mistakes were remembered and played upon so many times that people in many cases remembered his mistakes rather than his good deeds.

For Jesus, being thrust into a world so different to his own with the exact opposite teachings of his own with people having a completely different set of desires and expectations, could be imagined, to have been like someone who had only listened to ballet music all their life and then was suddenly introduced to a heavy metal concert with no exit doors.

Everywhere he looked, he saw chaos and disruption. He was not always able to get communication from heaven; many times he was shut out, unable to get any help or information, which also disoriented his thinking, and what was the reason for his visit to this strange place. As he became a young man, he was always being

THE ARRIVAL

challenged about who he was and what he was here for. He sometimes answered strangely, which was not understood by those questioning him. In fact, many times they attacked his words with hatred and anger, shouting, "How dare he say he is the Son of God!"

The servants of Lucifer knew their job, and that was to try to discredit this so-called Son of God so that no human would really care; in fact, Lucifer hoped that they would destroy this unwanted visitor. Although he did not want to do strange actions to show he had power and that he was from another place that governed the whole universe, he was challenged so many times that he actually did make sick people better, which no one else could accomplish, and many times, after they were cured, the people walked away, with little or no acknowledgment. Human behavior completely confused Jesus and further confused him as to why he was even here. He could not remember, at times, why he was here. His human side started to ask questions like, "Why should I?" "This cannot be right; how can I destroy everything here and go back to my home where I came from?"This type of thinking fell right into the hands of Lucifer, who was starting to enjoy the game. Lucifer had already planned his next several moves and had put in place his servants, who wanted blood in any way they could achieve. The people were starting to ask in greater numbers who this strange person was who taught such a beautiful doctrine, which was opposite to anything they had heard.

Also, this strange person was not afraid to say he was the Son of God. No other prophet had ever claimed such a title. They started to follow him wherever he went. Some even started to claim he would save the world and bring happiness and wealth to his followers. Jesus never offered such claims, but his followers decided that as he was the Son of God, he absolutely would save his followers. They started to claim this louder and louder till the servants of Lucifer heard the cries and began to consider him an actual threat.

The chosen tribes had also been watching all the fuss and sent several of their leaders to question this strange person and ask him whether he was the savior who would save the twelve tribes and unite the world under their banner. His replies, when asked over and over, were the same—that he would destroy the temple and rebuild it within three days. This was not understood, and most of the tribes could not or would not believe that the promised Savior, who had been promised to them for such a long time, would talk in such a way. They turned their back, claiming this guy was not their promised Savior.

While teaching, Jesus said things that were later distorted. Many humans used words from a text to suit their own desires or to confuse others enough to get them to believe them. When Jesus was asked to be king and rule this world, he replied that his kingdom was not of this world, that his Father's house had many rooms, and there were more wonders in heaven than this world could ever dream of.

THE ARRIVAL

Surely these few quotes show that Jesus was not interested in anything material, because it had no value in his Father's kingdom. Why would he even state such a thing if this world was of any interest to him? No, he tried to tell everyone that he was here to tell them about heaven, which could not be found unless the word about it was given.

In fact, many actually started to shun this fellow; they claimed that he was not for them and that he should be stopped from teaching such outrageous things. Lucifer was delighted, as he thought he was winning, and so he sent his servants to cause Jesus as much trouble as was possible. Some claimed he was blaspheming, and others claimed he could not prove his claims, but among his most loyal followers, Jesus performed many feats no other person has ever been able to duplicate. Even with so many signs of proof, many claimed they did not happen, or even if they did happen, they claimed it was trickery and instilled as much doubt as possible among his followers.

Many of his followers were so convinced he was the Savior that they actually wanted him to challenge the authorities and were willing to follow their King into battle. At this point, although the temptation must have been huge, he pointed out that he was here to save souls and that such an idea of conquering by force was not God's wish.

This could not be understood, as people did not understand Jesus was here not for the living; his mission was to enable all the trapped souls to always be able to leave this world in future without any constraints. Humans did not and could not understand that they were actually trapped in this world without any way to escape. They could only understand that they were living and believed that being saved meant being granted power over others, which was the strongest desire instilled in them.

When Jesus said this world was not his, they could not even consider the actual meaning. Some thought about his idea and felt it could be right, so they decided to follow him and his teachings to see what would happen. Mostly it was curiosity and not firm belief that made them follow, but some actually began to believe it strongly and started to suggest that others believe it too. The majority, however, could not accept that a passive way would be successful. What they had always wanted was complete control over their controllers. The idea of turning the other cheek when hit could not be understood. How would such an idea possibly save them?

The claim that the temple would be destroyed and rebuilt in three days was so far fetched from what they'd understood that all they could do was laugh and declare him a blasphemer. Again, this opposite thinking caused many to walk away; in fact, they began to look at this strange person as a fraud and someone who should not be followed. Lucifer was very happy, that he was able to use humans to get rid of this problem and so ensure that God could not destroy him or harm his powers. He had been thinking of ways to make sure this nuisance would

THE ARRIVAL

be weakened and had developed an invisible covering with which if anyone was covered, the person would not know it was there, and it made communicating very hard no matter how much power they had.

Lucifer had his most trusted servant put a very small package at the feet of Jesus while he was sleeping. The servant then quickly moved away to allow Lucifer to make the spell work. Lucifer then sent the spell to open the package, which flew up in the air and slowly floated over Jesus and engulfed him. Even when he woke up, he did not understand what had actually woken him.

He noticed, however, that his ability to contact his Father was becoming harder and harder, to a point that he started to think that no one cared and that maybe his Father was actually getting bored with this game. This started to cause anger and doubt, and clouded his direction and nearly made him want to give up and just return to his Father.

CHAPTER 22

THE TEST

With doubt and confusion starting to become a major factor, Jesus decided to get away from everyone to try to make contact with his Father and also to settle his thoughts as to why he was so confused. This feeling was so strong that he told his followers he would be away for a while and made plans to go to the quietest and desolate place he could find. He decided to go into the desert, as only a few humans were there, and he would try to contact his Father from there and ask for help. Lucifer was also watching this development with much pleasure, and knowing this nuisance did not know that he had a secret covering, he decided to follow him into the desert and watch what he did.

The first two weeks were uneventful, and Lucifer was annoyed that without any other distractions, this person could actually talk to his Father, but he was happy that it would be only for a very short period. The isolation

THE TEST

and quiet started to make Jesus tired and doubtful as to why he was even here. His human form was showing increasingly, and he seemed to be able to do nothing about it.

While talking with his Father, he was informed that he had a covering placed there by Lucifer, and he was told how to remove it without Lucifer knowing. The trouble was that Lucifer was watching, and the amount of energy required was such that he was totally exhausted. It was here that Lucifer appeared and tried to get Jesus to give into agreeing to worship him. He made three offers, all of which were rejected by a very tired and weakened Jesus. It was here that Lucifer was referred to as "Satan" for the first time. His name in heaven was "Lucifer," the second most beautiful and powerful angel in heaven.

However, Lucifer had always been referred to as a godly spirit, but now this was a name that did not recognize his position as a godly spirit. To the annoyance of Satan, he had to allow Jesus to leave. As Satan was unable to hurt this soul directly, he decided to go and plan other ways to get rid of this very annoying threat once and for all.

The interesting point here is that had Satan known exactly what was planned, he may have had other ideas about how to deal with this Jesus fellow. Jesus left the desert and immediately contacted his loyal followers, and after some food and sleep, he felt much better and stronger; in fact, he was feeling so good that any threats or doubts simply just left him. His followers also noted the huge difference and started to ask that he lead them to conquer the world with him as the leader.

This was not important to Jesus at this point. In fact, he was seeing his role clearly and would not listen to any silly human ideas that could in any way distract him from his mission. The more he said no, the more the humans tried to get him to lead them to conquer the world, and still he refused. By this time, the others were thinking that this person was becoming a threat to their very existence and decided it was time to get rid of this blaspheming phony who kept saying he would destroy the temple and rebuild it in three days. Who could claim such outrageous things and not be blaspheming?

In fact, it was surely time to make him confess that he was a liar or bring him before the court of the land to be charged as an impostor and blasphemer. He returned to his followers and explained that his time was near and that certain plans had to be completed first. Using his human instincts, he chose twelve humans to continue his work, naming a leader and claiming that this leader would be the rock and foundation to continue after he was gone.

He also told the leader that he would deny him, and another picked follower would actually betray him and cause him to be killed. They denied this, saying that they would follow him faithfully, but both their leader and the picked follower did do exactly as he'd said they would. Was this a sign for future generations that he knew all things past and future and wanted to give a message showing he does?

THE TEST

The leader was empowered so that whatever he bound on Earth would be bound in heaven and anything that he was loosed on Earth would be loosed in heaven. This command seemed OK if it had been issued in heaven. However, like humans, they did not understand its true meaning or power. These words or commands would help and excite Satan in ways at the time that could not even be imagined.

I will not delve into the details about what actually happened, as stories and folklore have already given many versions, but I'll just say simply, that Jesus was in fact, arrested and beaten to a point most would be dead by then. As planned by Satan, he was offered to the masses of people to be disposed of, who called for him to be crucified. He was then humiliated, whipped, spat on, given no food, and made to carry a cross heavier than his own weight. To make his humiliation even more degrading and complete, they decided to put convicted thieves on his right and left.

Now Jesus had to die to be able to complete his mission, which sadly was not known or understood by the people. His actual mission was to make an opening to allow all the souls to escape if they wanted and to be able to go to God's kingdom, heaven. It was an opening that no power could close and neither could any power prevent anyone from leaving through it if a spirit wanted to go.

This knowledge was kept from Satan and had Satan actually known the exact reason why Jesus did not fight or complain about his crucifixon, maybe the actual

WATER AND OIL

idea of a crucifixion would not have been entered in so quickly.

Jesus was crucified in front of many, and people did not understand why. If he was so powerful, why did he not just walk away or fly down and slay all those who were trying to hurt him? Surely if he was who he said he was, he could do what many asked, but they had no idea what his mission actually was.

Also, to confuse this story even more, as Jesus was losing his life and just before he actually died such a horrible death, his ability to contact his Father—who had been a huge help during his ordeal—was lost, for a very short time, he was dying like a human, a position he had never experienced, also when he was confused and feeling lost that he actually called out, wondering if he had been forgotten. This made some wonder, was he actually who he said he was?

Now you may say, "So that is the end of the story. What is so strange? It is just a little different in timing or information."

Maybe, but there is much more!

(Let me digress for just a moment and ask a question. You have a favorite Son, one who means more than life itself. You have to watch as this wonderful Son of yours is nailed to a timber cross and as huge nails are driven through his hands and feet. You watch this, unable to do anything, as his bones are crushed and as the nails are driven through his bones, yet he does not cry for mercy or ask to be saved. Your tears run down your face as you watch Satan laughing in the distance, knowing you cannot save your Son. What would be your first thought? All spirits have feelings, and I wonder if you watched such an event, could you, or would you, just forgive those who did this to your Son? There is more, but later would be a better time to discuss this.)

Jesus manages to complete his mission. Yes, he goes to space where all are trapped, and he makes an escape tunnel, allowing all those who want to leave a chance to do that. This escape tunnel can never be closed, so all the souls who go to this special space when they die as humans can now leave, but it is still a free-choice situation, so those who want to stay are free to do so. When Satan discovered the trick, he was furious, but he could not stop them from leaving.

After the opening was complete, Jesus leaves and returns to Earth to meet and show his followers that he has returned for a short time; they then get the strength to pass his words on to all the humans so that they can also know and make the choice to leave and join his Father's kingdom.

At this time the original idea was to, and in the future, leave decisions to humans, and further help or intervention would not be necessary. That idea was quickly discarded when it was noticed that humans were created with a follower's instinct, and without help, they would eventually fall again.

Many times interventions were granted, and at times when all was considered lost, help had been given to many humans. Even today, help is granted in many ways, from saving a life to granting wishes that were requested with deep faith in God.

Some humans have been given information about future events. Many messages were altered or changed to suit the teller because the original message was not properly understood. Some messages have never been repeated and were either destroyed or put in a place that only a few could ever find them, and even if found, the message would be old and not understood.

Satan, at this point, was furious that he was tricked and vowed that he would get full revenge on these humans who dared to even think that he was not the god of this earth and also vowed that Jesus would regret his visit and attack on his kingdom.

Jesus told his followers it was time for him to go, as this was not his world, and he would give those in charge some powers that would tell the other humans that they were telling the truth about his kingdom. He also instilled in them a strong belief that he knew, would not be broken easily by those who wanted to destroy them. However, Satan was also working fast to make sure any of these stupid humans who listened would be destroyed by other humans, and this would get rid of all these annoying humans.

CHAPTER 23

THE BATTLE

After Jesus left, Satan decided he should not rush into an attack, as any direct attack was now not possible. So he decided the best way to defeat this threat was to actually attack from within. At first, it seemed very hard, as no matter how many he managed to destroy, there were some who stepped in and took their places. Satan still had control of the humans he had used to trap this Jesus person. He decided the best way to defeat these humans and their desire to think of another instead of him was to make the desire to destroy any such followers so strong that they would make anyone who believed in Jesus run away and hide in fear. In time, they would see he was the only god and that all others were unimportant.

He planted desires to catch and destroy as many as possible and in the most horrific manner; then he felt they would all give up this silly idea of Jesus. Some were fed to lions, and some were used as practice for the army or were crucified as Jesus was, but they did not have any help as he did. This made death last longer and more painful. Some were beaten to death with sticks or rocks, and some were burned alive, but no matter how many were killed, there were still many ready to believe in this Jesus. Still determined to eliminate these troublesome humans, he devised more ways to stop the others following. The words Satan liked most about the teachings of what he called a weaker god were as follows: "What was loosed on earth will be loosed in my kingdom, but what laws you keep will be kept in my kingdom."

Using this as a guide, Satan slowly invaded the thinking of the leaders of this new domain. Greed was presented and shown; it was not only great but also gave pleasures not easily enjoyed by lesser humans. Also, all forms of pleasure could be obtained if people only thought about their personal pleasures.

This started to work, and slowly the leaders started to gain huge wealth and power, which they were not used to. The idea of so much power brought joy to the humans, who enjoyed being in charge of such a wonderful system.

Then other thoughts were introduced, which included every bad deed able to be committed by humans. Every command given by this Jesus was broken or twisted, to a point, that his commands really did not apply to the top but only to his stupid followers. Satan was pleased that he had actually won the bodies of these weak humans; after all, he actually made them love their desires, and so he was sure that he could win the battle that was started by Jesus.

THE BATTLE

As things started settling down, again Satan was not pleased that there was only a limited amount of trouble that a few humans would suffer. So he made a new plan, which would extend the bad deeds of these fools who followed such a lax system and actually wanted to think of God.

Money was being spent at such a fast rate that more monies had to be found, especially as the locals were being taxed to a point that they were starting to leave what was now called the "church." It was devised that certain powerful humans, who had become in charge of various departments, especially the financing, should suggest ideas that armies should be formed to spread the word and pay homage to the God of heaven.

So huge armies were assembled and sent out under the guise of Christian knights to attack any human who did not immediately submit to these new teachings. This pleased Satan very much, as it gave him another idea to use in the future. In the meantime, he ensured that the heads of this so-called new religion were made as corrupt as possible and made the teaching being presented look weak and a joke. The foundation of this new practice was established in a very solid way. What was not taken into account was that humans could be tricked into any misdeed that was presented. In fact, it became so easy for thoughts or ideas to be presented that it became a secret playground for Satan.

He made sure that every command regarding the basic teaching of this so-called Christian religion would be broken by the leaders and he also ensured that their deeds would be discovered by the common people. So good was this tactic of his that many people started to doubt the real meaning of what they were being taught. A few who would not be blinded by this behavior actually broke away from the main group and started to claim their beliefs were the correct ones and that humans should follow them. They taught the same basic teachings but said they were not in agreement with the behavior of others.

This pleased Satan, and he knew that each splintered or breakaway group weakened the original group, which gave him more chance to corrupt these smaller groups. He reasoned that if he corrupted all the groups, he would discredit God and then beat him into the ground, and consequently, God would lose the battle in his kingdom.

There was something Satan could not understand, and it was beginning to torment him. No matter how many of these humans he corrupted, for some reason there always seemed to be an army to keep following, saying these new teachings were right. However, as Satan surveyed his kingdom, he noticed that the number of these silly people who liked this new form of worship were starting to get smaller, and in fact, many were hiding and not making any noise that indicated they were the new Christians.

This was very pleasing to Satan; he began to relax, thinking the few left would soon give up and return to thinking about him as the one and only God. While all this was going on, Satan also realized that humans actually liked magic and would quickly follow anyone who could produce amazing feats, especially if money was involved, or a promise of power. So he went to his underworld and asked the spirits there, "Which spirits would like a chance to make these humans follow me more?" Many replied affirmatively but also said, "We cannot enter the world above without being called to appear." Satan replied, "I will grant certain humans the knowledge to ask you to appear, so you can help them."

It was agreed, so Satan carefully chose several humans and gave them the power to ask the spirits to help solve their problems. This power was meant to be limited to a few, and there were very strict rules that had to be followed in bringing the spirits up. Should mistakes be made with the special verses or if misread in any way, the control of the spirit could not be guaranteed.

For a while, it was working fine. The few to whom this information was given quickly developed large followers who were amazed at the powers that could be achieved. Quickly it was realized that money could be made quickly and power could also be attained if they allowed these spirits to help them. It did not take long for humans to try to cheat and steal the information for their own use. Some actually achieved their aims, but some, not knowing all the symbols or verses, quickly got into trouble. Some were attacked by the spirits and actually taken over, and some were actually killed, sometimes in the most horrific ways.

Some carefully made perfect copies of the ways to achieve this feat and made documents exactly showing how it should be done and hid them in safe places. While all this was happening, the groups of churches that had formed decided to make such actions evil and demanded such practices stop immediately, but this demand was thought issued in jealousy because they did not have such power, or it was reasoned if they did not understand it, they could not ban it!

These groups became larger, and the heads of the groups became rich and powerful. Such was their power over their followers that the followers would do anything to satisfy their masters. The controllers of these powers, in order to make identifying each power easier to understand, referred to the powers as white power or black power. These were modified over time as white magic or black magic. Some changed these slightly, but only the name was changed and not the use or intentions. Some claimed white power was for good and black for bad or evil, but both were basically the same because both used evil power to achieve the end result. Satan actually made the power unstable and unpredictable so that no person could challenge him or his power. They could only use this power in limited ways to seduce unsuspecting humans and give control to Satan. Small groups were established, where actual worship and obedience was demanded to be able to become a member, and this pleased Satan, because they were, in fact, worshiping him. These covens grew in size and numbers, each claiming more and more power for their members.

The small groups of churches challenged the use of such evil powers, but their protest fell on deaf ears, and actually throughout the world at that time, it spread at an amazing speed. During this time instructions were lost, changed, or modified for easier and quicker results, but sadly it also made the results more unpredictable, and in many cases, the result ended in tragedy for the user. This did not stop others from searching and sometimes finding those instructions in order to achieve the results they desired. Some became successful and kept it secret, and some could not understand the instructions and perished cruelly. About this time Satan realized that his power was being lost again to these small groups of Christians, who insisted on saying there was only one God in the universe, and that God was not on Earth but in heaven! As well as giving the power to select humans, thoughts were introduced to also have parties and celebrations to make humans even happier. So many celebrations were introduced that they became very popular, and all other ideas or thoughts were completely forgotten.

Some of the celebrations were so popular that humans would not stop performing the rituals no matter what. In fact, so popular did they become that the Christian followers decided to copy many of the rituals to try to get people to follow them. About this time, a huge conflict seemed to rise up, and the leaders had a problem they could not explain. In their enthusiasm and eagerness, they proclaimed one God and one creation, which was correct about the universe in general, but the "one creation" did not cover the Earth. Yet they explained the one God had actually created everything.

How to keep credibility and not change their initial claims yet still say humans had original sin when God was supposed to have created everything? How could God create something that had sin! So they covered their story by saying God created man and woman and that it was the woman who was led astray. Therefore, all humans who were descendants from the first two had to carry that mistake through history for generations.

How could it be explained that another spirit had created the humans and the world when they had stated very clearly there was only one God who created all things?

Yet how could the idea of original sin be explained when God created a perfect human to start things going?

God knew that humans in the world had been created by Satan and therefore would have great trouble entering his kingdom even if they knew about heaven. There had to be an explanation that was easily understood. In those early days and even today in many countries, the woman is considered to have a lesser status, and although modern times have changed many things, the woman is still considered lesser in status to the man. So claiming the woman naturally had to be the fallen one

THE BATTLE

was accepted very easily and never questioned by anyone, not even women.

At no time was this serious fall ever explained as to what the woman was supposed to have done, except eat an apple to get knowledge that God himself actually had. If that was a sin, surely every person who tried to get knowledge or improve themselves would be committing a huge sin!

Logic in today's teaching surely does not say, "You cannot get knowledge." In fact, the teachings from Jesus clearly states, "Search and you will find; ask and it will be given." They knew if they made it general knowledge, many would question their initial teachings and writings, which would be completely different, and this would cause much trouble.

Could this wrong story issued from the start be the reason many think the woman is to be blamed for all of humanity's problems? Is this why people consider her the cause of all the trouble that has always been on this planet? Is this maybe the reason the woman is considered to be below man because he was not tempted?

Humans have always been reluctant to admit mistakes even when the truth is presented, maybe through pride or fear, but many times throughout history, true stories have been retold in different ways than what had actually happened, or to suit the storyteller.

In fact, Jesus stated clearly he would rebuild the temple in three days, and he stated firmly that the temple would be built to replace the old, a completely new set of rules would apply! In other words, all the rules and teachings of the Old Testament would be completely replaced with the New Testament.

Yet even today many refer to the Old Testament as current reading, when, in fact, the teachings of the old would not be acceptable in modern times! Just to mention one point: "An eye for an eye" cannot be accepted today even by Christianity and its teachings or the laws currently in place.

The word "Sabbath" was taken from the Old Testament and referred to a message given to the Jewish people to observe. It was never stated by Jesus that worship to him was essential on a particular day. This was adapted for the church to make it important for humans to visit a place designated and be convinced that they should support their church because it was delivering God's word.

Only the Old Testament stated the Jews should observe such a day, which is a Saturday and not Sunday, but Sunday was chosen as a suitable day for making a rule to visit the church.

Also, it should be remembered that in the early days, it was considered essential for the church to have knowledge from all sources, be they good or bad, because this knowledge gave huge power to the church leaders, knowing exactly what was thought or what was happening. So confessions were devised to allow the church heads to gain information and a way to keep control of the

THE BATTLE

parishes by fear and guilt. The idea that such confessions were just between the priest and God was a suggestion introduced to make everybody feel secure enough to tell everything.

All information was demanded about all things even if they were not actually a sin, so to speak. The information was given in fear that God himself was listening and would know if a lie was being told.

The information, at times, was used to extract pleasures from the people to the great happiness of Satan.

Also, this information, at times, was not only used to obtain pleasure but also used as a way to make others do what was required, and if refused, the word "excommunication" was waved over the person's head, which made an immediate willing subject!

By commanding that confession was essential before communion could be had, it gave the church power to make sure everybody told his or her little inner feelings and deeds at least once a week. The reason was unless confession was performed, no communion was possible.

Jesus never demanded confessions or stated one had to confess before he or she shared communion or worshiped him, but it was commanded by the church, which even today is used as a control mechanism for controlling people. In fact, it was stated that the actual act of taking communion removed any sin, so why the forced demand?

Sadly, there are still today religions that prevent women from getting knowledge, and I ask a simple question: Except as a form of total control and complete dominance, allowing a man to do as he pleased without any resistance, why else would such a thing be enforced?

Could it be that God demanded all women to obey men's wishes completely, regardless of what he asks? If that was considered for even a second, how could we ever claim God is merciful and forgiving?

Could God have actually given such a command? Did God issue such an idea for a religion?

Now back to my story.

It was over six hundred years since this annoying human called Jesus had left Satan's kingdom. Yet no matter what Satan did, people seemed to be still considering this annoying person. So Satan again planned a scheme, which he was sure would upset these Christians as they called themselves. He decided to create a new religion that would challenge everything these so-called Christians claimed. It had to claim the same basic ideas but with subtle differences so as to trick even the most careful examination yet simple enough to be understood by many, without education and without any such knowledge, yet attractive enough to want to follow.

At the time the male was the dominating person in the family, and most tribes were judged by an elder, also a man, so it had to appeal to the leaders of the families. It also had to give control to the male and make his actions absolute.

This idea pleased Satan because his thinking was this: "Control the family, and you control everyone." Also, it meant that as the male was so proud and demanding by nature, his actions would be easily controlled. How to achieve such an idea was easy for Satan. Since he produced the humans on earth and basically had control of their emotions, he had a complete understanding of what they wanted and what their desires were. Also, he knew how to make humans do anything to achieve their secret desires.

The teachings devised by these annoying Christians started with the writings called the Old Testament, so these ideas were adopted, as the early teachings stated it was important to avenge any wrong done by others. So the idea was just copied and added so as to ensure attacking any Christians or unbelievers was justified. Also, other commands were added that approved using any force needed to expand the teachings.

This was already used by the early Christians as a way to expand their teachings, so again it was quickly adapted. Satan was happy because he believed his newly developed worshiping system would challenge the so-called Christians in his kingdom.

The Christians would send armies to conquer any who did not believe in Christ and any who did not understand. To Satan's pleasure, such people were also killed, some in the most horrific ways. Yet it did not matter; it was all good as far as the Christians were concerned. This idea of killing all who did not believe gave Satan another idea, and that was he would also include such an idea into his new religion. This would then challenge any Christian group that tried to establish itself, as both religions were similar yet different enough to see a difference. He used similar ideas and even some of the same names that the Christians used, but Satan also knew that any lie spoken often would be believed by many.

Lucifer also knew that only a few would even check the claims made, as many did not have the ability to do so, or such information was not available. He knew it would be considered a fact, and most would believe in what his established book said.

So a new religion was started, and with strict rules and very strict control over the families, Lucifer was aware that once established with his support, he could expand and keep control of many of its leaders. So you could say the battle lines had been drawn, and Satan's ability to challenge this new idea called "Christianity" could be defeated and even discredited if he was persistent. The way to firmly make challenges was to make sure his religion was established close to and right in the face of those he opposed, the Christians.

At this point, it must be remembered time was of no consequence to either God or Satan, as times counted by humans' life was a mere thirty-five to sixty years at that time, if lucky, which was like a quick flash to Satan. So what was planned, say, for five hundred years, could not even be imagined by humans. Being aware that humans, no matter the reason, would change and alter any information given, to make sure the information actually was a benefit. Also, Satan had witnessed many messages sent that had been completely distorted, because the message could not be explained, but more importantly without changes would show little benefit to the messenger of the message.

During this initial stage, the Christians were requiring more money to build churches, pay for elaborate desires, and to be able to indulge in their favorite amusements. This required more and more money, so to satisfy these needs, armies were established to go and, under the name of Christ, plunder and ravage, sending the spoils of these so-called wars back home, to the great pleasure of the leaders and Satan. This was then spent sending others even further into the new world, to find even more treasures to feed this everlasting hunger for money and power. Wars were waged in the name of Christ, and many were either converted to this new belief or were met with a quick dispatch to another place.

The distances between where these beliefs were first established and the places to control or conquer made controlling and conquering so very difficult that power started to be shared not willingly but by both sides and it is interesting that with the additional help offered by Satan most victories were short and bloody conflicts where both sides suffered great losses, but the Christians were mostly denied long-term possession.

The truth is that no Christian victory lasted very long in this faraway land, even in human time, except for a single area, which was reclaimed at a much later date, but only a very small area, which I will return to later. Yet most of the fighting and demands were in the middle of this area, and even today it is still in the middle of the conflict, with both sides saying they have the right. Yet after nearly seventeen hundred years of disputes still raging, no solution seems even possible. Because humans think very slowly and changed their mind quickly, it allowed Lucifer to observe and infiltrate the inner circles and plant and change ideas and offer extra seduction temptations to a point that few even realized what was happening until it was either too late or the physical pleasures were too great to stop.

Satan also was able to copy the method God used to send messages to his followers, and he found these followers were so anxious to receive messages that regardless of the message, the recipient of the message did not question or doubt whether the message was from God. In Satan's eyes, he was the god of this earth.

This was a huge advantage, and if results are examined with this information in mind, it would be discovered that many messages given and acts ordered were wrong, many times with very bad results, to the joy of Satan. His easily tricked humans who dared to go against him. After all, it was his kingdom; he controlled it and he was sure he would absolutely beat this annoying God into defeat.

At this point, it should be remembered that with all the beauty and ability Satan had, he still had a huge fault. He is a proud spirit, both beautiful and powerful only next to God, so his powers in his kingdom are absolutely

THE BATTLE

huge. He is able to instill doubt, jealousy, anger, wars, desires, and every sort of damaging act into his realm to achieve his goals. Also being most likely still mad at being cast aside, he is also full of anger, revenge, and probably all the emotions that go with them.

CHAPTER 24

THE CHALLENGE

Lucifer now had the idea and the means to develop a system that would feed his desires to destroy all the humans who believed in this annoying Christian God. He carefully picked the human he wanted to start opposition to this Christian belief of only one God because as far as Lucifer was concerned, he was the only god who needed to be paid attention to.

A person was chosen, one who was quiet and thoughtful but also very susceptible to ideas or thoughts. He waited till the right moment came and appeared to him while he was meditating. A set of reasoning was presented with just enough conflicting information that even the most doubtful person hearing such a message would believe it was from God. The interesting thing is that Satan deceived him. Information was extracted from early teachings, making sure it was just enough to confuse but agreeable enough to be quickly accepted by the people. As mentioned earlier, Satan has a huge fault, and that is that he is very proud; he would make sure his name was mentioned many times.

Happy with his work, he then set about making sure as many people as possible knew and understood this new teaching, which would challenge this Christian belief. He enlisted all his followers to spread the word and make sure all the men understood the message that his word was, in fact, God's word and that his chosen man was the boss and should control all things.

Realizing that man also had to have discipline or he would not agree, to just doing something without a reason, strict rules were established to make sure his basic desires were covered. A mix of Christian beliefs using early Christian beliefs and some old god's that were familiar to the people but altered just enough to encompass the basic desires of man was just what was needed to trick humans into rejecting the other beliefs. Even the establishing points were close to and, in fact, nearly on top of these other people's sites who had dared to cause Satan so much trouble.

While all this was going on, other divisions were appearing, both from the early Christians and the group that was originally chosen by this Christian belief as the chosen tribe. The Christians were starting to disagree about how they should teach the teachings from God and the others were starting to break up into several other tribes each claiming their interpretation of the teachings were the right one and all should come their way. This pleased

Satan so much as he thought he was already winning and believed it was just time it would take to win totally.

In fact, all around the world, there were contradictions and arguments as to who was right and who did not understand the true teachings of God. Others were becoming scared that their followings were going to others who were offering more pleasures and monetary gains. So what was to be done?

It was decided by some that the only way to discourage belief in such evil ideas was to brand anyone who did not agree with the church's teachings as heretics and devil worshipers. Should anyone know of these evil persons, they were to announce them to the church leaders, and action would be taken against any who practiced witchcraft or any magic spells.

People were seized and tortured until they admitted they did such things; others denied until they were either dead or so unable to talk they were just let go quickly to their deaths unable to say anything against the church. This brought great joy to Satan, who loved such treatment of humans and planned even more ways to increase the pain of the victims, enabling even more information to be extracted, and it mattered not whether it was false or true or even made up as long as it stated it was against the church.

Think of it this way: If a church cuts you to pieces and torturers you in a way that cannot be described because it is so barbaric that it would not be believed, would that person have any love left for God? When Lucifer presented himself to a dying person as a beautiful angel it

THE CHALLENGE

would be impossible for that person to believe it was not God, as we have all been taught that the devil has horns and is an ugly piece of work!

If an influential person did not like another, all he or she had to do was whisper the name, and that person was arrested and tortured until they admitted the so-called accused crime and then all property and money was taken to the pleasure of the church. This did, in fact, initially reduce the ability of some small witch groups and others to operate, and many slipped away to become secret groups away from the church's eye and made the leaders of the churches believe they had won.

Yet even today there are secret societies that openly praise Lucifer and ask and get powers granted for agreements to serve and adore Lucifer. The major problem, however, was that many writings and instructions were destroyed, making the ability to use the magic ineffective, and so many either joined others or lost their followers because they could no longer use their magic powers. This gave the church a way they could in future control any group that in any way went against the church's ideas or teachings.

The new religion established was growing larger by the year, and, in fact, it had already spread to many areas outside the church's influences to a level Satan was thinking he could win easily against this invisible force that had run away from his kingdom.

Satan decided he needed even more confusion, so he again started to sow ideas that were against this annoying religion, and he planted other ideas in the leaders' heads that they should even get more power and riches and the best way to do that was to expand their area by wars and demands and get the treasures returned so that added benefits could be enjoyed by the leaders. This idea was welcomed by the leaders, and so again, armies were dispatched in the name of God to expand the influences of the mother church. It is common knowledge that the churches demanded more and insisted that more power is given, to a point even the kings of countries would not go against what the churches demanded or asked.

CHAPTER 25

THE EXPANSION

Lucifer's new religion was expanding at a very fast pace, and he was now so sure he would be able to defeat this annoying God; he believed that all he needed was time, which he had plenty of.

The area he chose was really perfect, as it was next to where he had arranged the death of this annoying pretender to his kingdom. And the people wanted to believe in a God but had no teaching as to what or which God to believe, as already there seemed to be many to choose from. As all the other gods had been created by him, so really there was only one that had to be defeated.

The seeds of deception had been set, and by this time, news had reached the head of the new Christian church that another pretender to God's throne had been established. To be sure, it was necessary for the church to defend this holy ground where Christ was crucified, and that an army should be sent immediately to protect the holy land. This was done, but as was the case to be repeated many times, the army was defeated, and it returned home bloodied and without any prizes for the Holy See.

This was exactly as was planned by Satan. "Let them send armies to be defeated, and in time, the idea of defending such a faraway wasteland will seem pointless." This allowed the new religion to flourish without any distraction, as the other occupiers were too small a number to cause any lasting problems. Things progressed as planned, with some small delays, but, generally, wars were being fought, and leaders were being corrupted, especially in the heart of his enemy, the so-called church. The greater the corruption, the greater Satan's pleasure.

He even created serious divides, making several leaders claiming to be the one in charge; in fact, many had referred to them as "antipopes," showing just how successful his planning was. It pleased Satan to be able to create so much corruption, because if the leaders were corrupted, then it would, in time, do the same to the followers, and then he would be the eventual winner. Some of his chosen, who managed to get to the top, were so corrupt that Satan thought he would win quickly, but there always seemed to be some individuals who came at the wrong time, which delayed his plans. But generally, he was very successful with the ones he chose.

God was watching what was happening in this lonely kingdom and realized that Satan was trying to make it possible for the humans to travel into the darkness of space with a possible idea to attack heaven with destructive weapons. Satan had not forgotten the trick played on him by that Jesus person and promised he would get revenge no matter what.

So over the centuries, and so very slowly so as not to cause alarm, this Earth has been moving away from any kingdom created for God's faithful followers, so as to make it absolutely impossible for any human to even consider the possibility of contacting others in his kingdom.

Also with the limited life-span given to humans, the ability to travel long distances is basically impossible. Space travel, as we understand it and with humans' inability to travel faster than light, makes reaching even the closest possible area that could support life impossible.

It has only been discovered recently that space is farther than thirteen billion light-years from this planet, and that is not the end. In fact, the distances are far greater than anyone on this earth can even imagine, but in spirit travel, even long distances can be achieved quickly, as it is covered in a completely different form with great speed.

There will be some at this point who will argue that science and mathematical equations claim it is impossible to travel faster than light. Their expressions would be correct if applied to this planet; however, away from this planet and in different forms, such travel is absolutely possible.

Because this message is not about what is or is not possible, it is not the time or place to explain the constraints binding this planet's inhabitants, or what is or is not possible away from the bounds of Earth.

Just accept that away from the physical limitations here, many things are possible, and amazing discoveries will be offered when it is time for each to go.

Do not forget that Satan created this kingdom for him to be the god, and he is also the second most beautiful angel, only next to God himself. So his ability to be seen when he wants to be or just enter people's thoughts or create dreams or ideas is very easy for him.

Remember Christ returned from being crucified and appeared to many before he decided to return to his Father in heaven, so it shows the ability of such powerful spirits to achieve what they want. Many, when they die and Satan appears, think he is the god, and they immediately give praise and want to be with him. With this thinking, they have no desire to search for another place but to stay content with the vision of Satan. These poor souls will only be enlightened when the time comes and the God of the universe actually returns to this planet. Again, I ask, if he did create this planet, why is there such a claim that he would return when the last days are near? What would be the reason?

Like a god with slightly fewer powers than God himself, Satan's ability to create is also limited when compared to God's. For example, according to our best scientific brains, approximately five billion years are left for Earth's existence. The sun has also been here for a similar time, yet should the sun stop sending warm rays

THE EXPANSION

to Earth, we would quickly freeze, and all life would die. We are told the sun, like Earth, has also about the same life left, about five billion years, so it seems, even judging by scientific explanations, that the sun's life has a time limit.

That calculation states the sun now will lose most of its power in another 4.5–5 billion years' time. However, its actual life is not what is important. What is important is when will the sun's rays fail to give enough light and warmth to this planet.

Even during a full eclipse, which is a few minutes, the Earth loses about ten degrees of heat. So should the sun's warmth drop even fifteen degrees, this planet would experience huge changes, and that may be even enough to stop this planet from working as normal.

At that time, a prediction has already been given, that the end of the earth will come, at a time when all will be in darkness and God will return to gather any spirits left who want to be with him. I have said it several times—if we believe the story, why would a God who created this planet have to destroy it to save the souls he supposedly created?

"Wow!" I can hear the comments. "Such a long time to go?" However, spirits have no time limit, and as we have been told many times, an end will eventually come, but we do not know when the Earth will actually end. If the sun for any reason failed to keep the hot light coming here, this place will freeze like a block of ice, along with everything in it.

Suffice to say that each person who dies, it is the end of the world for him or her, so forgetting the huge time span the Earth can survive, each human's time here is between a few minutes to maybe around a hundred years, with some maybe a little longer, after which they will experience an end to this world.

To back up what I have said, God of the universe has no time limit and no limitations as to how long something can last. In fact, he claims "forever with me." So what should we believe—forever or a limited time only?

That does not seem the case with Satan, who is limited to a time frame, and his time to challenge seems to be limited to about the time it is decided the end will come here.

Again, it may be stated that is a very long time, but compared to the universe, we know even ten billion years is not a long time. We are only just discovering the huge distances that space covers and have little or no idea how far it actually stretches, but maybe as time progresses, our understanding of ten billion years is a short time in spirit calculations. As already stated, we have measurements of over thirteen billion light years away, and we are still finding ways to see even further.

Back to our story.

About this time, Satan realized he had more work to do, as again he seemed to be losing power. The church was becoming more powerful and had started to see Satan as a powerful enemy. So stories were made up of him having an ugly tempter who wanted to take all the humans to the depths of hell and who looked like a monster with horns and would destroy anyone who was bad and keep them forever locked up in a dark, terrifying place never to see light again.

Their idea was to scare people to a point that the mere thought of doing anything but what the church stated would scare even the most stubborn souls to behave and do what they were told. This idea worked for a long time, and the church even devised the thought of excommunication as an additional threat to keep everybody inside the church walls and teachings.

The threat of being banished to darkness when they died was a terrifying thought. In fact, so powerful was the fear of this devil that paintings, stories, warnings, and as much fear as possible was developed to make sure all followed the teachings of the church and were in absolute fear of this unseen devil and what this devil might be able to do, should they not do as they were told.

Mistakes were blamed on this unseen devil; any misdeed was blamed on him. But because they did not understand what they were teaching, it was, in fact, falling directly into Satan's hands.

The reason was, when they actually died, they had an understanding the devil was, in fact, a two-horned monster who wanted to boil them all in oil. When a beautiful spirit presented itself, they could only relate that to God and immediately thought this must be the one and only God! This made Satan so happy that these stupid humans, who thought they were so clever, we're doing exactly what he (Satan) wanted.

Divisions were starting to develop in this Christian religion as some were starting to decide their ideas were better suited to what they wanted to believe, so slowly small differences became much larger differences, which were at first fractures, and then doubts started to divide even the most sincere members.

The main church was also having trouble with money and decided to make sure their teachings were being followed. So letters were sent to senior members to check on what was happening. Very soon, it was discovered that many early followers had left in favor of worshiping others and, in fact, had actually found ways to gain wealth by worshiping Satan and his spirits.

With little knowledge, except a direct desire for power and with only one goal, they started to chase these lost souls and bring them back to the church.

An order was issued that if anyone practiced these forbidden forms of worship, he or she should report them to the church for cleansing. This idea pleased many, as all who had enemies or people whom they just disliked reported them to the church.

They were then tortured in the most horrific ways until they admitted what they did to the great pleasure of Satan. This was so successful that it was put into the teachings that any person who worshiped anything except what the church taught would be arrested and taken to the dungeons for cleansing.

This also had a huge political advantage, as anyone who opposed the church's teachings would be brought

THE EXPANSION

before the church and made to confess anything to gain power. Such power had never been wielded before; with a threat of excommunication for devil worshiping, it gave the church huge powers, at times even greater than the kings of those times.

The church again started to gain power and riches. On the other hand, its costs also increased. So more money was demanded to keep the money flowing to the church. So much power did the early church gain that even kings sought the churches' approval before making decisions. This again gave the churches great power.

It was time for Satan to get back to work, so he started again to give wild suggestions to the leaders, who at times accepted his ideas completely and carried them out. Planning was made. But for that more money was required. So more territories were needed to support the plan. So it was thought why not send more armies to the motherland and possess the land conquered by the followers of Satan?

This idea was easily accepted, and armies were deployed to expand the areas of Christianity so that more wealth could be brought into the church.

So crusades were started one by one, each bigger than the last, and all had one mission—that was, to get the gold, silver, and carpets by any means. People could kill or get rid of anyone in their way. These crusades were quite successful in the beginning and brought great wealth to the church.

The pendulum however quickly went against these self-proclaimed Christian knights as the local tribes dealt devastating defeats and huge financial losses to the church which although it never quenched its desires but did prevent further excursions venturing into their lands.

However, the local tribes hated any idea of worshiping such a hateful God represented by these Christians and happily accepted the new idea given them which today has a huge following and yes in many ways is showing they dislike Christians very much and would like to destroy any people still trying to say they are Christians.

CHAPTER 26

CONFUSION AND DOUBT

For centuries, the church has used fear, threats, demands, altered information, and false teachings to make the people believe that anything the church said was the truth. Those who disagreed with the so-called demands of the church were said to be wrong and very evil.

The idea that any power that could not be seen or attributed directly to the church is either just a myth or maybe even inspired by Satan and so it should not be believed or even considered because it could be a possible trick by Satan, is what the church claims.

Whenever books, letters, instructions, or anything else, that criticized or claimed powers against the church, it was destroyed, and the writer was killed or tortured or imprisoned until death. Even today, the church has messages and information given by messengers of God that have been kept secret, and they still refuse to divulge those messages.

For many generations, this deep-seated belief perpetrated upon people by the church not only influenced their understanding about the world they live in but also reduced it completely to zero so much so that anything outside what people could directly experience or understand seemed totally evil.

The idea of dragons and powers outside normal abilities have been claimed to be either trick's or inspired by evil. Because such abilities and most of all the information about them has been completely destroyed, teaching future generations that there were powers far beyond anything the normal human could understand was and still is considered to be just impossible.

The truth is that many of the ideas about other forms of life, whether with the ability to fly or just create what appeared like magic to others, were not just some thoughts of the writers. Many of these ideas were, in fact, from others' experiences or stories told to them over many generations, because writing such stories would have meant death.

We have been taught since childhood that these make-believe stories are only for children; actually, could they be true. Out of humanity's fear of such things, they've been confined only to children's stories. Humans seem to be cursed with a gene that makes them want to destroy anything that is different or that cannot be understood, without any desire to try to understand the discovery.

CONFUSION AND DOUBT

Even the movies that tell of life beyond our ability to travel, beyond known areas or even communicate with the unknown depict destruction or elimination, so any human who notices anyone or anything that is different decides destruction to be the first choice and then maybe, to find out the details of who or what it was. Unusual sea creatures caught or seen are destroyed, if possible, and the dead creature's picture is then plastered all over the media showing a monster or alien fish but always dead. It is almost an afterthought to check and see what it is, with the excuse that we are doing it for science.

About the things shared in this story, they'll be those who say, "Unless I see actual records or pictures, what is being told is just imagination." These folks want proof that a dragon existed or that extra powers can be achieved. It might be suggested that early paintings by ancient masters could be proof that they existed, but many would still say that it is only an imagination.

This is not a new demand, because even two thousand years ago, the same demands were being asked from the person most Christians claimed to be the Son of God. Today, many will still say, "Yes, he was absolutely. But maybe he did not do everything that they said or the stories have been exaggerated, so why believe what I do not understand?" If you believe that a person is the Son of God, could that person have any limitations as to his abilities? Should any force or person be present today claiming the same thing, like, "I am the

Son of God," I venture to say the same treatment would be meted out again, only this time with more cruelty to make crucifixion seem like an easy death. We are taught that God created this world, but not which God! If the God we believe in created a world, would he not know what he was creating? Is there any doubt that he would put people into paradise, knowing that they would fail on the supposed first temptation? Where is the belief in an all-knowing God—one who not only knows the future but has the power to create any situation he desires? Can it be believed that such a God was playing games and, in fact, knew they would fail, thus giving an excuse to banish them away to what could be referred to as hell when compared to the paradise they were in?

Is there any logic that a God presented as a loving and caring God would sit back and enjoy what the Earth has developed into?

If logic is applied to any of the past wars or the past history or what is currently happening, which is little different to the past, could all this be attributed to a loving God? We are taught God will forgive, but if logic is applied, God would only create peace-loving situations and surely could not be blamed for the suffering of humans ever since they appeared on this planet.

I can only wonder how the humans were tricked into believing such a loving and powerful God, would even be considered possible of creating suffering just to get some to believe in him when he was supposed to have created everything!

Why would it seem logical for a God to send his Son to die a horrible death with the excuse the humans need saving if he, in fact, created the humans in the first place?

These questions surely cannot be brushed aside like many questions with no answers with "That is God's desire or plan."

There is again no logic why such questions have not been answered truthfully, and that is either because the church has hidden the answers for their own gain, or sadly they do not have the answers! Many times when the church is asked a simple question that they can't understand, they give the standard answer: "A mystery of God; do not question his will."

Yet on many occasions, Jesus clearly stated, "Look, and you will find; ask, and you will receive." Why would such a statement be given directly by Jesus, yet the church still cannot answer these questions but only hides behind the statement, "That's God's will" or "That's God's mystery, so just accept it"? The history of most churches claiming to be the true church has been, for hundreds of years, simply using the institution for their Leaders personal gain and pleasure from humans who believe their stories.

The rituals celebrated by churches today use parts of or, in some cases, are the same rituals referred to as "satanic rituals" that have been copied so that the people would accept them and come to the churches. Isn't it realistic to conclude if they were created purely by God for his people that copying others would not be necessary?

Especially rituals created by the only enemy God has in the universe?

Why would a heavenly God need to create many gods for humans and then completely reverse and demand humans should only have one God before them? How can it be accepted that God allowed Satan in a place in his kingdom? He banished him from heaven and yet gave him access to his creation, Earth.

Does this have any logic to it? Logic surely shows Satan was here first, and, in fact, the church starting way late had to accept what the people already knew to get them interested in the new church. If all this was created by our heavenly Father, who is the creator of the universe, why would we call him merciful if all that he supposedly created did nothing but kill rape, and commit every forbidden command given by him? Could it not be suggested that if this was the sole domain created by God, he would indeed banish any evil found in his kingdom as he'd already done with Lucifer in heaven?

Why would God need two kingdoms? Isn't one enough—his heaven? Can anyone claim that heaven created by God is filled with hatred, killings, struggle for power, desire for money and possessions, and every evil that God says is wrong? Then how can it be even suggested God created such an evil planet so that he could watch the humans suffer from the excuse "When you die, I will bring you to my kingdom"? Surely, this does not make any sense.

CONFUSION AND DOUBT

So it seems logical that coming here and allowing his Son to come here to be challenged, humiliated, and ultimately crucified is different to what we have all taken as the right story and more importantly what we have believed as the right reason.

Jesus actually states very clearly, "This world is not of my kingdom." Why such a statement if all was created by him or his Father? Surely, such a statement would only have merit if he or his Father had no hand in creating this world, and the reason for coming was to try to save the human soles created by another?

I ask these few questions to maybe awaken a new thought that maybe the humans have been tricked for over two thousand years and because a wrong story was first created and developed for the benefit of the people controlling the churches that after so long how to correct a basic misconception.

This story is not intended to fight or criticize the idea that there is a loving God and that paying homage to him is right, but it is only to confirm that yes, there is a very loving God who suffers greatly watching humans suffering and is very limited in what he can actually do at this time.

The Tower of Babel is a story about humans wanting to get to heaven with the wrong idea, and that was to be able to attack heaven. It was watched by God, who, when the tower grew too tall, sent his angels to destroy man's ability to attack heaven and limit any future attempts to be able to ever do such a thing again. The story says God changed the languages so as to prevent such a happening again, but my story says Lucifer changed the languages so he could control the humans better.

Why would such a tower (or means) be destroyed, if God actually created this planet? Maybe the reason was God knew it was Lucifer's way to attack heaven, and God wanted to absolutely prevent any such happening then or in the future. Remember the story of the dragon being tricked? Maybe that was a way to explain the story to me so others would understand it better.

There is little actual scientific proof because an actual starting point of this world is not available, but it is known that Earth is actually moving farther away from other planets, racing at sixty-eight kilometers per second. Yes, per second. If looked at for just one year it would be approximately 2,138,572,800 K. If you look at only a hundred years, the distance covered is amazing, and if you multiply that by only a million years, just sit back and say wow!

Imagine you had a new house and your friends came to visit, would it not be natural to show the house and all the rooms to your closest friends? Why then would an all-powerful God create a kingdom filled with mysteries and many unanswered questions. When asked about him or this world, we are given a simple statement, "Oh! That is a mystery of God"! Surely, that does not make any logical sense!

Because religion has been used as a control mechanism by the ones to whom the power was passed to and because fear has been used as a means to control, using the words "hell and damnation" if one doesn't submit. The average human has been indoctrinated into submission, believing what they have been told.

This fear has been used for centuries to demand a complete surrender to all the teachings claimed by churches. Humans have accepted such demands regardless of reality and sometimes due to the physical and financial hardship they endured, all in the name of "I have the power, so just do it, or else eternal damnation to all who do not surrender."

In all the teachings given by Jesus, there is no demand that money should be given prior to being able to have some returned. There is no demand that prior to receiving communion, one has to have "confession." The feast days are mostly decided by churches and used as a way to control the humans, as the church says you must come. Moreover, many celebrations have been altered, and everybody agrees that most of them were related to Lucifer or even strange-sounding gods but all created by him.

Today a hot subject and watched by millions are movies relating to vampires and spirits that are nearly all impossible to dispose of but have magic powers not only to live for a thousand years but who can come back from the dead and attack, anyone they please or are commanded to. There are stories of killing them by putting a stake through their hearts, burying them upside down so they could not climb out of their coffins and many other instructions available about such creatures.

Are you aware that the first vampire information is described as being over four thousand years ago along with possible ways to protect people from these evil spirits brought from the underworld?

It is also interesting that describing such spirits either being summoned or released from the underworld does also indicate that they were, in fact, real and such powers also existed long before Christianity was introduced to this place called Earth.

Could this also give strength to the story that even today we are intrigued by the possible idea of bad and uncontrollable powers being able to just arrive on this planet and we love the stories because they are only stories, but are they?

During this story there seems to be a slight contradiction, the story says the spirit has a free exit should it be wanted after death. Lucifer has the ability to grant favors providing he is worshiped and after granting the wishes asked for, the spirit is with Lucifer maybe never to be given freedom. So it seems each has the ability to choose, but depending on which path is chosen, may depend on the spirits ability to leave, or maybe its desire to leave is blocked by Lucifer as a way to seal the agreement.

A story told; is about a spirit called Mephistopheles who is bound to Lucifer and is Lucifer's servant, who tries to warn Faust not to give in to human desires because he did and now can never be released. Is this a warning?

Our story does also mention very clearly it is a choice to leave that is the key to leaving, but if that choice is blocked by an agreement maybe that could change the terms referenced as free choice.

The interesting position currently is the Christian church although at this moment has a greater number of followers by a small margin, compared to other forms of worship, it is actually predicted they will be second in followers possibly within ten years or less.

The other confusing idea suggested by some, is that Christians have referred to God as Allah in the past, this is however only stated by others wanting to cause doubt but the reality is, this point is wrong. Only two religions have ever used Allah as a reference to God, and the ones who do, actually believe Christ was only a profit for God. Christians have never used this term for God.

Jesus stated many times he was the son of God and his kingdom is and always will be forever an actual statement. No other person since records have been written has ever stated such a claim. Only people who are trying to copy or confuse and maybe cause doubt have tried to give the impression of being forever but none except Jesus has ever stated they are forever.

As asked earlier is the idea of original sin told because Lucifer has created all the humans and his stigma or identification is marked on every sole created which must be removed before entry to heaven can be granted?

Is this the real reason Christ insisted all be baptized?

Also to be remembered is Lucifer, although his time is limited, does seem to be catching the greater number of soles at this time which begs the question, can it be asked is Lucifer actually winning the battle for soles here on Earth?

Another interesting point I would like to mention is even today power is achieved by leaders who have the largest following and the more humans that vote or support a leader, that leader becomes much more powerful. Presidents today or leaders who gain the full support gain amazing power, just look at China or Russia who's power is gaining strength daily, and compare that to the Western world who's leaders are weakened by conflict and divisions, there power is weakened. Does this sound familiar?

The actual essence of this story shows it has nothing to do with wealth, power, status, or any material item on this planet. It is an actual battle between two powerful spirits that have a challenge, as to who can win a battle for the soles. Surely this point shows God did not create Earth but is trying to inform and save the souls here from eternal darkness; which he knows will come, and sadly he is also aware that the soles here do not know or understand the consequences of being complacent.

At one time, I did not agree or understand the story I've just shared with you. For a long time, I just kept it within me and pondered about it, but it kept nagging, so after a lot of checking to disprove such a story and having been unable to, have decided to ask for your opinion to see if you also agree.

The rest is up to you!

CHAPTER 27

CONCLUSION

May I ask some simple questions: If you believe that a person is the Son of God, could that person have any limitations as to his abilities?

If we do not understand the reasons or actions done by others, does that say their actions never happened?

We are taught that God created this world but not which god!

If the God we believe in created a world, would he not know what he was creating?

Why would he create a world with a confirmed limited life yet say his kingdom is forever?

Is there any doubt that he would put someone in a paradise, knowing that he or she would fail on the supposed first temptation?

Do you believe God of the Universe would allow celebrations to him using rituals created by the only enemy

God has in the universe and who he already banished from his kingdom?

Is there any logic that a God presented as a loving and caring God would sit back and enjoy what the Earth has developed into?

If logic is applied to any of the past wars or history or even what is currently happening, which is little different to the past, could all this be attributed to a loving God?

Why would a loving creator have everyone he was supposed to have created, be born with sin?

Could that sin be actually the mark Lucifer made when he created humans which would maybe block soles from entering God's Kingdom?

Why would it seem logical for a God to send his Son to die a horrible death with the excuse the humans need saving if he, in fact, created the humans in the first place?

Why would a heavenly God need to create many gods for the humans and then completely reverse and demand humans should only have one God before them?

It is common knowledge that many old gods were claimed as satanic, so how could any logic be applied that they were created by the God of the universe when he says clearly "do not have any false gods?" So it seems logical that coming here and allowing his Son to come here to be challenged, humiliated, and ultimately crucified is different to what we have all taken as the right story and more importantly what we have believed as the right reason.

CONCLUSION

Jesus actually states very clearly, "This world is not of my kingdom." Why such a statement if all was created by him or his Father? Could it not be suggested that if this was the sole domain created by God, he would indeed banish any evil found in his kingdom as he did with Lucifer already from heaven, so why allow him back?

Thank you for reading my story and I hope it stirs questions for you as it has for me.

www.ingramcontent.com/pod-product-compliance
Lightning Source LLC
LaVergne TN
LVHW021821060526
838201LV00058B/3469